The Authentic
CUBA
Travel Guide

Christine Williams & Julian Hatfield

Copyright © 2016 by Don't Forget To Move. All rights reserved. No part of this publication may be reproduced, distributed, or transmitted in any form or by any means, including photocopying, recording, or other electronic or mechanical methods, without the prior written permission of the publisher, except in the case of brief quotations embodied in critical reviews For permission requests, email the publisher, addressed "Attention: Permissions for Cuba eBook," at the following email address: contact@dontforgettomove.com

ISBN: 9781520243283

DEDICATION

Without the people of Cuba opening up their country and their hearts to us, this book wouldn't be possible. We give thanks to their warm hospitality, the doctors at the dengue hospital and that little Cuban lady on the corner of Picola and Acosta for the amazing pizza!

Contents

Introduction	7
Why Travel to Cuba (with a Brief History)	9
When to Go	12
Cuba With No Spanish	14
Obtaining a Visa (with Extra Info for US Travelers)	17
Currency: A Tale of Two Economies	25
What's Up With Cuban Food?	27
Where To Stay	32
Transportation	42
Budgeting for Cuba: From Low to High	49
Safety in Cuba	60
Traveling as a Solo Female	65
Traveling as a Solo Male	71
Traveling as a Couple	74
Avoiding Scams	76
Getting Sick in Cuba	84
How to Find Internet	90
Must See Experiences	95

Bonus Extras

Cuba Travel Hacks	107
Havana Walking Guide	115
Thank You	126
About the Authors	128

Introduction

Back when we first visited Cuba in 2013, there was limited information online about this mysterious country. We had vague visions of Cuban cigars and Havana Club rum, classic cars, and beautiful beaches. And while all of these are quintessential Cuba, the country is so much more than these iconic symbols. From the moment we entered Havana in an old beat-up Chevy packed with locals and tourists alike, we felt like we'd hit on something special. Before even venturing into the city, we knew our two-week stay wouldn't be enough time. So that first day we went directly to the *Cubana de Aviación* (Cuban airlines) offices and extended our trip by another two weeks. We weren't sure if it was the energy in the streets, the beautiful crumbling architecture, or the city's magic, but we were instantly smitten.

Luckily for us, our gamble paid off and our first impressions of Cuba were spot-on. Nothing will compare to our first visit, where we did everything in our power to have the most authentic experience. We soaked Cuba up like thirsty sponges, speaking to locals every chance we got. We took local transportation: dump trucks fitted out with upholstered seats and buses full of long wooden benches. Every experience, no matter how far out of our comfort zone, was an opportunity to delve deeper into the mystery. To our surprise, Cubans were very open in voicing their opinions on the country. They expressed their views on Cuba's complicated history and uncertain future, often inviting us into their homes to share their personal experiences. These personal encounters gave us a better understanding of the local culture and a deeper love for the destination.

When we returned in 2016 to write this guide, we had a very specific vision in mind…to show people the *real* Cuba. It's no secret that Cuba has become one of the hottest travel destinations over the past few years. Now that restrictions have been loosened for United States (US) citizens, it's only going to become an increasingly popular destination. After decades of restricted travel, Americans can now fly directly from the US to Cuba. But that doesn't mean travelers should be worried about Old Havana becoming a strip mall with a McDonald's and a Starbucks on every corner. Cuba is still a communist country and, if the last fifty years say anything about Cuba's progress, it's that change will be slow. But as travelers start to come in droves, there will be a greater chance of tour companies selling a prepackaged, sugarcoated "Cuba experience" for a pretty penny. Just as with every other tourist destination, you'll have to put some effort into getting off the beaten track to get a taste of the real Cuba. That's why we wrote this guide: So you can get the most out of your trip and see Cuba in all its rich, vibrant, complicated glory. Because if there's anywhere you want to experience authentically, trust us: It's Cuba.

Why Travel to Cuba + Brief History

If you are reading this, it's safe to assume you're interested in traveling to Cuba. You've seen the photos of classic cars rumbling down the street, of Cubans puffing away on giant cigars, and of pastel-colored houses lining cobblestone streets…and you're ready to go! But first, we'd like to paint a picture of present-day Cuba and explain why it's important to go now.

Before we mention travel, let's briefly discuss the history of Cuba. There is a lot of history to cover, and depending on how far you want to go back, it gets a little messy. Alternating between liberated, independent, liberated, and independent seems to be a common theme for the country, between Columbus showing up in the mid-fifteenth century and present-day Cuba.

In a very brief recap, all you need to know is that since the success of the Cuban Revolution in 1959, Cuba has been a socialist/communist country up until present day. During the 1960s, this didn't sit well with the US (and capitalists), so the US imposed an economic blockade on Cuba, which also severely limited Cuba's ability to trade with other capitalist countries. Although Cubans still had trade with the Union of Soviet Socialist Republics (the USSR) and its allies, they were significantly limited in what they could import.

This left Cuba in the "time warp" that everyone commonly refers to. In many ways, this is correct. Cuba has been left in a state of economic limbo over the last sixty-odd years, especially over the last twenty-five years since the collapse of the USSR. Since the early 1990s, Cuba has struggled economically. As a country, Cuba is aware of the developments happening in the outside world, but they're unable to achieve them because of harsh political constraints (imposed both internally and externally).

Enter the 2000s. Cuba has begun to realize the advantages of opening up to the world. The first change happened internally as the government began to ease restrictions. Private business (home stays and restaurants) started to open up, Cubans got cell phones and the Internet made its way to the country (albeit very slowly). Now fast-forward to 2016: The US and Cuba are actually communicating again. President Obama became the first US president in more than eighty years to visit Cuba; the Rolling Stones performed a concert; and US to Cuba travel is all but legalized.

Now more than ever, Cuba is opening up its doors to foreigners, and undeniably it's going to have a positive economic effect on the country. You may have heard a lot of people say things like, "Get to Cuba before it changes" or "I want to go before they get KFC and Pizza Hut." And although this logic is true, the actual reality of it is a little further away. Cuba *is* opening up to the world, and the changes *will* inevitably come, but they won't happen overnight, which is all the more reason to get there *now*. Now that we've covered the boring history lesson, let's continue our adventure through authentic Cuba!

Cuba History Resources

Here are some other easy reading resources to get you started on Cuba's fascinating history. They range in facts and political bias. If you're interested in knowing more there are a ton of resources out there that talk about Cuba's unique history.

Cuban Explorer (covers geography, history, etc.) - http://cubaexplorer.com/brief-history-of-cuba/

History of Cuba (everyone's favorite research friend Wikipedia) - https://en.wikipedia.org/wiki/History_of_Cuba

A Brief History on Cuba (little US centered, but a 2 minute read) - http://www.localhistories.org/cuba.html

Christine Williams & Julian Hatfield

When to Go

There really is no bad time to visit Cuba, but every season has its pros and cons. Besides deciding when you can take off work, you should consider two important factors for choosing travel dates: weather patterns and tourist crowds. Ideally, you want to travel through Cuba when the weather is at its best and the crowds are at their smallest. Unfortunately, these two things rarely happen at the same time, so you've got to be strategic about booking a trip.

In Cuba, the dry season runs from December to April and has the best weather of the year. These months have less rain and are also relatively cool and fresh, with much less humidity than in the summer months. Remember, it's the Caribbean, so you're still going to work up a decent sweat, but it won't be as bad as the rainy season. Because the weather is best during this time, it's also the peak season for tourists. Expect more crowds as people try to take advantage of cooler temperatures. June to August can also be peak months for tourists as most of the northern hemisphere enjoys summer vacations. During these two periods of high season, you can expect crowds, higher prices, and less availability for accommodations. August does have a brief dry spell, but is also commonly the hottest and most humid month to visit.

Wet season runs from May to October and, apart from June to August, this is the low tourism season. You may have to deal with unexpected downpours, although these usually only last a couple of hours. It's also particularly hot during these months as the humidity rises, especially in June. You'll be sticky with sweat and the rain won't do much to cool you down. Luckily, most hotels and shops have air conditioning, and you actually get used to the heat. Just be prepared to look like a hot, sweaty mess during especially warm days. It's okay: Everyone else is just as sweaty as you!

There is, however, a plus side to traveling during the low season. There are fewer tourists, prices are lower, and it's much easier to find accommodation. You do run the risk of some hotels and resorts being closed for the season, but you won't have any trouble finding alternatives. You can also score some great deals on tours and activities. September and October are hurricane season, but chances are you won't hit anything too bad. Keep an eye on weather warnings before you depart.

Weather varies between regions and usually gets hotter the further east you travel. Over in the eastern capital of Santiago de Cuba, expect weather to be hotter than in Havana, and you won't get a nice oceanside breeze. If you plan to keep to a certain town or area, look up specific weather information: It may be different than the rest of the country.

Christine Williams & Julian Hatfield

Cuba with No Spanish

One the biggest concerns for travelers going to Cuba is the fear of not being able to speak the language. Although the vast majority of Cubans don't speak much English, those living in the big cities tend to speak more and you'll find that many working in the tourism industry are almost fluent. If English isn't your primary language, you can also find many translators in popular tourist areas, especially around Havana. In other popular spots like Trinidad, Santiago de Cuba, and Varadero, you can find translators located around the tourist centers or near the main plazas. Just don't expect your average Cuban *campesino* (farmer) to bust out fluent German if you end up lost!

When you step outside of the tourist areas, you're less likely to find someone who speaks decent English, or any language besides Spanish. Cubans are super-friendly though, and even if you can't directly communicate with them, they are patient. Body language and a little bit of impromptu miming goes further than you'd think! But if you really don't know any Spanish, no worries. You won't be expected to learn fluent Spanish just because you're visiting Cuba. All you need is a couple of key phrases that will make things a lot easier when trying to communicate. To get a head start on your Spanish skills, check out *Duolingo*, available as a free phone app or online. It's a great language resource that can help you learn a bit of

Spanish before you go.

If you don't have time to get your head around the grammar, a quick online search will help you find some great lists to get your started. FluentU.com has most of the basic phrases you need to learn in Spanish, including pronunciation hints.

Alternatively, you can grab a good dictionary app to save yourself walking around with a big book all day. We personally recommend the Collins Dictionary English-Spanish app.

Besides the basic Spanish phrases, some Cuba-specific slang may be useful to help you up your street cred with the locals. Here are a few to get you started.

Qué bolá? / Como anda? − (pronounced kay bowl-la/ co-mo ahn-duh) It's like 'what's up' or 'how you going' in Cuba.

Jinetero/jinetera − (pronounced hin-e-ter-o/ hin-e-ter-a) Generally refers to a sketchy person up to no good. For a male it might mean a street hustler trying to catch you up in a scam or con. For the women it more than likely refers to the different kind of street hustler trying to catch you up in a bit of 'fun'.

Frutabomba − (pronounced as it looks) is what Cubans call papaya. In most of Latin America the word for papaya is the same, but in Cuba it's slang for a woman's vagina, so try to avoid asking that female fruit vendor about her *papaya*. It could be a little embarrassing.

Yuma- (pronounced you-ma) referring to a foreigner, especially a white skinned/ blonde hair person.

Gua-gua - (pronounced wah-wah) A small bus frequented by locals.

Obtaining a Visa + Extra Info for US Travelers

The number-one concern for travelers visiting Cuba is how to obtain a tourist visa. Although traveling to Cuba is restricted only for citizens of the US, it can still be confusing to understand which visas are needed for other nationalities. Note that restrictions on US citizen entry into Cuba come only from the US government. The Cuban government is more than happy to welcome Americans into the country.

Aside from citizens of nineteen lucky countries, almost every person traveling to Cuba will need a visa, which is also commonly known as a tourist card. A quick Google search will let you know if you're on the visa-exempt list, but anyone from the main tourist locations of the US, Canada, western Europe, Australia, and so on will need to get a tourist visa before landing in Cuba. At time of publishing, Cuban visas cost the equivalent of $25 US dollars (USD) and are usually very easy to obtain.

What's the Difference Between a Visa and a License?

A Cuban visa is what most travelers need to enter the country. Also known as a tourist card, it's a small piece of paper on which you fill out your basic details, such as name, address, passport number and date of birth.

A license is required only if you are a US citizen traveling to Cuba from the US, or you are a non-US citizen who is traveling from the US. Technically it's not actually a license and there is no physical piece of paper. There is also no application or fee and you don't need any proof to obtain it. The license is only a form that you fill in that details the reason you're traveling to Cuba, based off twelve specific travel categories. More information can be found on the license and the twelve categories later in the chapter.

Visas for Non-Americans

If you're not traveling to Cuba from the United States, you won't have to do anything difficult to prepare a visa. Most likely, you will receive your Cuban visa at the airport check-in. For some airlines, such as Air Canada leaving from Canada, your visa will be included in the ticket price and you'll receive it after boarding. Because each airline is different, your safest bet is to check with your airline or travel agent immediately after booking to see whether you need to secure a visa before flying, or whether you receive your visa on the plane. Each company does things differently in terms of Cuban visas, so it's important to speak to a representative directly. If you are flying from the United Kingdom (UK), Thomas Cook and Virgin Atlantic should allow their customers to pick up the visa from the airport. Otherwise, you may need to contact the Cuban consulate in your home country. If your airline doesn't issue the visa, and you don't know how else to get it, there are agencies that will send you a visa in the mail for a fee. If you do need to have a visa sent to you, apply right after you buy your airline tickets to ensure you will receive the visa on time. Depending on your nationality and the time of year, you may experience delays in receiving a visa.

Here is a list of sites that organize Cuba visas if your airline doesn't:

- Cubavisas.com
- Cubacenter.com
- Cubavisa.net
- Cubavisa.uk

Most countries are permitted a thirty-day tourist visa with a possible thirty-day extension. Canadians can stay in Cuba for up to six months, but must apply for an extension before the ninetieth day. Once the extension visa is issued, it's valid for 180 days.

Christine Williams & Julian Hatfield

Visas for US Citizens and Those Traveling from the US

If you are flying to Cuba from the US, no matter what your nationality, you will need to organize a visa before getting on the plane. You'll also need to choose one of the twelve categories for Cuba travel, which gives you permission to enter Cuba legally (detailed later in this section). The visa in the US is often distributed at the airport by your airline and can be paid for and filled out on the spot. Major airlines that fly directly from the US such as JetBlue, Southwest, American Airlines, and others will have a visa ready for you at the airport. However, it is always best to call your airline ahead of time to confirm the company will issue one at your particular airport. If your airline does not supply the visa, you'll need to get one from the consulate in Washington, D.C. or contact an agency, such as those listed previously, to purchase one. As US to Cuba travel continues to improve, this process will no doubt become smoother. Already most US airlines are providing the visa before departure, so it's likely this won't be an issue.

If you are flying from the US, no matter your nationality, you will also need to select one of the twelve categories of Cuba travel in order to get a license (not a real license, just permission to enter). Technically, US citizens traveling from anywhere in the world should always be traveling to Cuba with a license under one of these twelve categories, but it is not policed, enforced, or anything more than a dated technicality. Whether you're a US citizen or traveling through the US, there is no physical process you need to go through to obtain a license. It's completely self-licensed and there's no paperwork you need to fill out or apply for. When you are at the airport you will be given a piece of paper with the twelve categories and you simply choose the one that applies to your situation. No one will ask you anything or ask for proof. This is completely based on the honor system. It is unlikely you will ever be asked which category you fall under and much more unlikely you will be asked to provide evidence. This is a bit of a gray area and sort of middle ground between fully banned travel and lifting the restrictions entirely. Still, it's a good idea to have a category in mind just in case.

To reiterate, if you're from the United States, whether you're flying from the US or passing through a gateway country, you must qualify for one of these twelve categories to get a Cuba travel license. This applies to non-US citizens traveling from the US as well. Here are the official twelve categories from the US government:

- Family visits
- Official business of the US government, foreign governments, and certain intergovernmental organizations
- Journalistic activity
- Professional research and professional meetings

- Educational activities
- Religious activities
- Public performances, clinics, workshops, athletic and other competitions, and exhibitions
- Support for the Cuban people
- Humanitarian projects
- Activities of private foundations or research or educational institutes
- Exportation, importation, or transmission of information or information materials
- Certain export transactions that may be considered for authorization under existing regulations and guidelines.

Which Category Do I Fit?

The list of motives for Cuba travel is extremely broad and it would be pretty difficult not to fall under one of the categories. Although technically you are supposed to be licensed under one of the twelve categories, there is NO official application process, check-up, or anything that would require you to actually present proof. That's not saying it's legal to lie about your reason, but you're not going to be prompted for any proof. We'll let you be the judge of how to

> handle this situation. "Support for the Cuban people," is pretty vague. Surely you're supporting the people when you stimulate the economy by buying sunset mojitos, no?
>
> If you are from the US and don't feel comfortable putting yourself in a category, you can go with a "person to person" tour company. These tours legally take Americans down to Cuba under the banner of "educational activities." This is a perfectly legal, albeit expensive, way to visit Cuba if you don't mind being on a tour.

Once you arrive in Cuba, the immigration officials will usually ask you whether you want a stamp in your passport or on your tourist card. Avoiding a stamp on your passport will ensure you don't have any issues coming back to the US. Of course, if you're flying directly from the US, having a stamp in your passport is not a problem as you'll have obtained the travel license (not an actual license) when you filled out your visa. We flew from Mexico and Christine (a US citizen) got her passport stamped. When she flew back to the US via Mexico, she wrote on her immigration card that she had visited Cuba. The immigration officer in the States did not ask about her visit to Cuba, nor was she ever asked about which of the twelve reasons she had for traveling there. This is the same for everyone we know who has traveled to Cuba.

It's not an ideal system for Americans who are looking to visit for tourism purposes only, but US citizens may feel more comfortable knowing that prosecution for Americans visiting Cuba is basically nonexistent under the Obama administration. It is unknown if travel restrictions will be reinstated by future administrations, but that's only one more reason to visit Cuba sooner rather than later.

Note that American bank cards still don't work at Cuban ATMs. This will hopefully change in the near-future, but for the moment, Americans will need to bring cash to Cuba. There is also a ten percent fee for changing US dollars into Cuban currency. Abolishing this has been proposed, but not yet confirmed. To avoid the fee, it's best to bring cash in a different currency to Cuba, such as euros, Canadian dollars, or Mexican pesos.

Americans should not feel nervous about visiting Cuba. Despite a tumultuous history between the United States and Cuba, the majority of Cubans welcome US citizens with open arms. They are happy to have our tourism dollars and most enjoy exchanging information and discussing Cuba-US relations. US citizens should feel comfortable visiting Cuba.

Currency: A Tale of Two Economies

If there's one aspect of traveling to Cuba that you should get a handle on before visiting, it's the money. Just to make your travels a bit more interesting, Cuba has *two* currencies. It is incredibly important to know the difference between the two so you don't get scammed.

The first is the Cuban Convertible, or the CUC (pronounced *say-ooh-say* or *kook*). This currency is always equivalent to the US dollar (1 CUC = $1 USD), so it's easy to remember its value. Most tourist prices will be listed in CUC, including hotel and *casa particular* prices, most restaurants, tourist activities, and souvenirs. If you plan on splurging in Cuba, chances are you'll mostly be using this currency.

The second currency is the Cuban peso, or the CUP. This is usually referred to as *peso* or *moneda nacional* (national money). This currency is worth a fraction of the CUC, about 25 CUP (1 CUC = 25 CUP). The peso is more often used by locals. You'll see prices for things like street food, public transportation, and some corner stores listed in CUP. It's important that you don't confuse the two: The last thing you want to do is pay 5 CUC ($5 USD) for something that is really worth 5 CUP (20 cents). Most Cubans are pretty honest and will tell you you've made a big mistake, but it's best not to test this.

Both currencies have their own set of notes and coins. It's pretty easy to tell the notes apart, but all those coins blend together and look the same after a while. Be on the lookout for the special 3 CUP (12 cents USD) coin that has the face of Che Guevara on it. People in the tourist areas will try and sell you them for as much as $5-$10 USD, but you can easily attain one by using local currency in the street to make purchases.

For a long time, there have been rumors that it's illegal for tourists to use the local Cuban peso. This is completely false. When you change your foreign currency into CUC at one of the money-changing houses, also known as *cadecas* (pronounced *ka-deck-as*), you can change your money into CUP at the same time. Simply take the majority of your cash in CUC and then take 20-30 CUC and ask the teller for *moneda nacional*. Remember: You'll need a passport with you to change currencies. No matter your budget, we recommend getting a mixture of the CUC and CUP. You'll likely come across prices in both currencies. Because of the high difference in value, it's generally easy to work out whether a price is listed in CUC or CUP. Have a close look at the money to make sure you're not getting hustled when you receive change.

Note: American bank cards still do not work in Cuba. You can change US dollars at the *cadecas*, but they will add a 10 percent fee. Your best bet is bringing euros or Mexican pesos to exchange. Non-American bank cards should work, but most ATMs only accept Visas. If you want to use a MasterCard, you'll have to withdraw money inside the bank, with ID.

What's Up with Cuban Food?

Ahhh, Cuban food…it's both a blessing and a curse in our opinion. On the one hand, you can find some super budget eats on the street, but the variety is fairly limited and the quality isn't very high. On the other hand, food in restaurants can be pretty expensive, at least by Cuba's standards. While you may find some tasty meals in the increasingly trendy restaurant scene of Havana, the food is usually pretty hit-and-miss. Here are some easy tips to finding decent food in Cuba.

Street Food

If you want to eat cheap in Cuba, it's very easy: Street food is abundant in every city you visit. Unlike a lot of other countries that serve up food from street-side carts, in Cuba, street food is actually sold from family houses. What you'll find is open doors and windows serving a variety of simple foods, including pizzas, sandwiches, and spaghetti. This food is incredibly cheap. Pizzas generally cost about 40 cents, fried egg sandwiches 10 cents, and spaghetti around 50 cents. You can easily eat in Cuba for a couple of bucks a day.

But before you get your hopes up, the street food isn't that great.

It's made with low-quality ingredients. (How else do you think they make 40-cent pizza?) It's greasy and unhealthy. Sometimes you'll find pizza with a variety of toppings including vegetables, but more often than not, it comes with just cheese and a thick layer of oil seeping from the sides. You can find delicious street coffee (dark and sweet) and sometimes yummy homemade yogurt or milkshakes. Occasionally, you'll also find larger street food operations that serve a meat or fish and rice dish with salad. These can be as cheap as 20-25 CUP ($1 USD) and are surprisingly decent for their price.

Note: The area around the University of Havana (in Vedado) is great for off-the-beaten track low-cost street food. Students frequent these spots throughout the week and they're also great places to meet locals and hear their opinions on contemporary Cuba. Another great location for cheap food options is around Marina Hemingway.

Paladares versus State-Run Restaurants

In Cuba, a *paladar* (pronounced *pal-uh-dar*) is a privately run restaurant. These range from family operations serving food out of houses to fancy, upscale dining establishments. Until the 1990s, it was illegal for Cubans to privately run restaurants, but now they're very common. Although the diversity of food in Cuba is somewhat lacking, the increase in privately owned restaurants has brought a resurgence of the culinary scene in Cuba. Here are some top-rated paladares located around Havana.

San Cristóbal - https://www.tripadvisor.com/Restaurant_Review-g147271-d2042638-Reviews-San_Cristobal_Paladar-Havana_Cuba.html

Atelier - https://www.tripadvisor.com/Restaurant_Review-g147271-d2373205-Reviews-Atelier_Restaurante_Paladar_en_Habana_Cuba-Havana_Cuba.html

La Guardia - http://www.laguarida.com/en/

Otramanera - http://otramaneralahabana.com/en/

Le Chansonnier - http://lechansonnierhabana.com/

Visa Mar - https://www.tripadvisor.com/Restaurant_Review-g147271-d1151869-Reviews-Paladar_Vistamar-Havana_Cuba.html

Corte del Principe - https://www.tripadvisor.com/Restaurant_Review-g147271-d3968188-Reviews-La_Corte_del_Principe-Havana_Cuba.html

---

The state-run restaurants vary in quality, but tend to be a bit dated in their décor and menu. Sometimes state-run operations offer food at a highly subsidized price, including ice cream parlors that literally sell scoops for pennies. You can buy a whole plate of ice cream for 5 cents, with special extras like syrup and fruit only 10 cents extra.

Cuba as a Vegetarian or Vegan

We're not going to lie, being a vegetarian in Cuba is pretty difficult. Meat, especially pork, is a staple in most Cuban dishes, so you have to be a little creative. With street food, your options are limited, but it's not impossible to find vegetarian options. In tourist restaurants, it's a little easier, and they are usually happy to be creative and whip something up for you. Finding a good variety of nutritious foods is more difficult, but for a couple of weeks, it's manageable. Fish is widely available, so pescatarians will have an easier time than strict vegetarians.

Traveling as a vegan in Cuba is much more difficult. You'll have to spend a little more money and/or speak decent Spanish to find meals without Cuba's favorite ingredient…cheese! If you're going the budget route, it's good to know ahead of time that there is a lot of dairy in the street food. The pizzas are usually premade, so finding a cheese-less option will be difficult. You can order the 10 CUP (40 cents) spaghetti and ask for no cheese, but honestly, the cheese is about the only thing that makes it edible.

For vegetarians and vegans alike, restaurants may be your only sanctuary from the torturous grasp of Cuba's obsession for meat and dairy. One tasty option is the typical dish of *congri* (rice and beans with spices), often accompanied by a side salad and *tostones* (fried plantain). Strict vegetarians should be aware that the beans are often cooked in lard.

You can find fresh fruits and veggies in different markets and street carts. These are great for nutritious snacks on the run or to take back to your casa to whip up a salad. A pound of fresh guavas or bananas will cost you no more than 50 cents from the various street fruit vendors that you find on the backstreets of Havana. Vegetarians and vegans may also want to consider packing easily transportable non-perishable foods. We usually travel with a tub of peanut butter, which is perfect with 1-CUP (4-cent) ration bread rolls.

Snacks

Those who prefer snacking throughout the day rather than eating large meals may have a tougher time in Cuba. There are a limited amount of snack foods, especially healthy ones. You won't find large, well-stocked supermarkets in Cuba. In fact, the stores that you find are pretty bare or only carry a very limited selection of items. Imported name-brand snacks are available in the occasional tourist shop, but are a lot more expensive than they are back home. If you are a big snacker, we recommend bringing granola bars or trail mix with you.

Christine Williams & Julian Hatfield

Where to Stay

There are many different accommodation options in Cuba, depending on whether you want a really local experience, or prefer the comforts of your own hotel room.

Casa Particulares

Forget Airbnb: Cuba is where room-sharing started! Private businesses have always been limited (or nonexistent) in Cuba, so instead of small hotels and bed and breakfasts, Cubans rented out rooms in their homes. This type of accommodation is commonly referred to as *casa particular* and you can find these rooms all over Cuba. You can distinguish a *casa particular* by the small sign that looks like a blue sideways "H" near the door. These will range in price and comfort level, but generally, you'll receive a simple room with *en suite* bathroom in a family house. If you're traveling on a budget, you can often find cheaper rooms with shared bathrooms that are just as nice. Basic *casa particulares* come with basic amenities such as towels and soap. If you stay in the nicer rooms, you'll often get a fridge, TV and A/C. It's also common for the hosts to offer breakfast and dinner service for an extra fee.

Traditionally, when Cuba had limited or no Internet, there was no way to book rooms online. Instead, you had to rely on the highest-tech equipment available at the time: the Rolodex. Nowadays, there are more options for booking online, but the Rolodex network is still a good way to book your accommodation. Here's how it works. After arriving at your first accommodation stop, the hosts will sit down with you, help you plan the itinerary for the rest of your trip, and then tap into their Rolodex of contacts throughout the country to put you in touch with your next casa. When you arrive at the next town, those owners will call ahead to the contact on your next stop and book ahead at that casa, and so on as you make your way through Cuba. It may sound outdated, but this is the original booking system in Cuba and the incredible network of contacts is a testament to the resourcefulness of the Cuban people.

Casa particulares are a great option for any budget. Rooms can range from $10 a night in low season to $50 and up in high season, with averages around $25. The nicer rooms will generally cost more, but the pricing doesn't always correlate to comfort level. In fact, similar rooms in the same casa may end up costing different prices depending on the guest. An older, wealthy-looking couple may be charged more for the same room than a group of young backpackers. There isn't a set price list posted in the casas, so they will quote you a price depending on the season and how much they think you'd be willing to pay. Haggling is definitely acceptable, especially if you are staying more than one night. We often reduced a $20 rate to $15 or occasionally $10. It's not about trying to undercut them or cheap them out of their money, but there is a reasonable expectation that you can haggle for your prices. If you think you're pushing too hard, you probably are.

> **Pro budget tip:** A general rule of thumb is that whatever you paid in your previous *casa particular* is how much you should pay in the next one if they refer you to one of their contacts. If you feel like you're paying too much, it's best to nip it in the bud early. Another way to combat price confusion is to ensure your previous hosts helps you negotiate the next rate before you arrive. That way, you won't have any problems and you can confidently pay the price you were quoted. If your casa won't budge on the price, it's likely they'll have a contact in town that will accept a lower price, perhaps further out from the city center.

Another scam to be aware of: When you arrive in a new town, opportunistic casa owners may try to persuade you to come to their house by telling you that the casa you reserved is closed or that they're actually the owner of the casa you reserved. If your Spanish isn't very sharp, it can be easy to think that the kind-faced lady ushering you towards her house is actually your host. There isn't anything malicious about it, but if you don't come prepared, you may end up at the wrong place and paying more than you should. Always get the address of your reservation beforehand and preload

Google Maps so you know exactly where you're going. (Yes, Google Maps does work in Cuba, as do other map apps.) Casa owners will often offer to meet you at the bus station when you arrive, so be sure to get their names ahead of time so you can ensure you're meeting the right person. If in doubt, ask to see a business card from their casa to confirm their identity, or ask them who your previous host was if you've been recommended to them.

Beware of the Illegal Casas

There are such things as illegal *casa particulares*. They aren't necessarily dangerous, but they do operate outside the government control. In Cuba, every casa has to officially register their residence/business and pay tax to the government on each guest they receive. These legal casas will have the blue sideways "H" sign outside their door and can advertise their services. Unregistered casas won't have a sign or name and are prohibited from hosting guests. The illegal casas generally cost less than a normal room because they don't need to pay the tax, but that shouldn't be an incentive to stay in them. These are not only illegal for the owner, but also the guest. Your best bet is to always stay at a house with the proper sign.

Booking Casa Particulares Online

You can book casas online through several sites, including Airbnb, but someone always takes a cut of that booking. The cheaper casas are not likely to be on a booking site, so if you're on a tight budget, we recommend waiting until you arrive to book. You can always find a room, but it is harder in the high season.

If you are arriving in the evening or at night, we recommend booking ahead so you're not wandering the streets of Cuba at night looking for a room. This is exactly what happened to us when our flight was delayed coming into Cuba and we ended up in Havana at 1 a.m. without accommodation. This is a testament to how safe Cuba is: Anywhere else, we would have been nervous entering a capital city at night with all our belongings. Not in Cuba. We gladly accepted the help of a local family that brought us into their house while the father ran around the neighborhood looking for a vacant room for us. After a cup of coffee, some conversation, and a lot of curious interest from the neighbors, the father returned an hour later, telling us he'd found someone just a few blocks away. Only in Cuba!

> **Here is a list of sites where you can book a *casa particular*:**
>
> http://www.cubaparticular.com/searchcasa.asp?Lang=0
>
> http://www.cubabookingroom.com/
>
> https://www.mycasaparticular.com/en/lodging-where-cuba-cuba-is/
>
> https://www.cubaincasas.com

Benefits of Staying with a Family

One of the best things about staying in a *casa particular* is the opportunity to interact with a Cuban family. But just to be clear, this isn't a homestay. You're not obligated to spend time with the family, nor are they obligated to spend time with you. It's pretty much like staying in a private room at a hostel, or renting a room on Airbnb. Although you don't have to interact with the family, some of our favorite memories of Cuba have been made while sharing a *Cuba Libre* (rum, lime, and Coke) with a friendly family, chatting about the history of Cuba or the Revolution. Some of our greatest insights into Cuban life have come from casa owners, who are usually very open about discussing their opinions on the country. With such an interesting history, and the people's voice being unheard because of technology restrictions, it's fascinating to hear their stories about Cuba. They are also happy to prepare home-cooked meals for their guests for a small fee. Like rooms, food is priced on a sliding scale, depending on your haggling ability, Spanish skills, and how well-off you look. We found meals in casas for as cheap as 1-2 CUC, but know other people who paid upwards of 8-10 CUC. For 3-4 CUC, you can get a delicious fish dinner, accompanied by rice, fried plantain, salad, and fresh guava juice. In the mornings, you'll find all types of fresh fruits and juices with fried eggs, bread, and honey for about 2-3 CUC.

Hostels

With the abundance of *casa particulares* throughout the country, hostels are still relatively uncommon in Cuba. They are becoming increasingly popular, though, and you can now find hostels with traditional dorm-style rooms, especially in Havana. It might not be anything special, but a bed in a dorm room can range from as little as $5-10 USD a night. There's also the possibility of getting a discounted rate on a longer stay. If you're a solo traveler, hostels offer a much better social scene than you would normally find in a casa. Hostels will have common spaces and provide a much better opportunity to meet people. If you're traveling solo or want to make some new friends, a hostel could be the way to go, although they are few and far between outside of Havana. If you're traveling with a partner or friend, it may be more economical to stay at a cheap room in a casa.

Here are our recommended hostels:

Hostel Hamel: Hostel Hamal was the very first place we stayed at in 2013 when we arrived in Havana. Back then, it was only 5 CUC a night. Now, the price may slide depending on the season. The hostel owner, Magnolia, is a really kind host who sat down with us and helped us plan our four weeks in Cuba. She pulled out her old Rolodex and found cheap casas for us all over Cuba. The rooms are simple and there's a common area that is usually busy with travelers swapping stories over rum. You can contact Magnolia via Facebook at: https://www.facebook.com/magnoliahamelhostel/

Ilé Ache: Ile Ache is a new hostel in Old Havana that we stayed at in 2016. It offers clean, simple dorms with a small kitchen to cook in. The hostel also provides free eggs and bread, so you can whip up a simple breakfast in the morning. A bed costs just 10 CUC a night and is a great alternative if you want to meet people along the way. This hostel is also in a very central location (it's only a ten-minute walk to the main tourist hub of Old Havana), but far enough away that you don't get all the crowds. Book at: *https://www.facebook.com/cubaturismoalternativo/*

Hostel Casa Caribe: Casa Caribe is a popular hostel in Havana with fantastic reviews on TripAdvisor. Rodolfo and his family are gracious hosts and are willing to accommodate whatever you need. A delicious light breakfast is included. You can find this hostel by searching on TripAdvisor.

CouchSurfing

CouchSurfing *(https://www.couchsurfing.com/)*, a popular website that connects hosts with travelers to offer accommodation in their house for free, does exist in Cuba. However, due to strict laws surrounding hosting guests, CouchSurfing is illegal. Both hosts and guests face repercussions if caught. Additionally, some hosts on the site may be charging guests to stay at their house. If you are looking to meet locals, but don't want to risk staying at an illegal accommodation, look for CouchSurfing events that connect travelers and Cubanos. Searching for Havana events on the CouchSurfing site will provide you with more detail.

Hotels/Resorts

If you're looking for something more private or upscale, there are plenty of hotels in the main tourist cities in Cuba. Prices vary from mid-range to high-end and really cater to the tourist market. It's not only the rooms that are more expensive: Expect to pay tourist prices for drinks, meals, and amenities too. Some hotels and resorts are quite beautiful, but others may be lacking in amenities or facilities. Many places in Cuba don't have access to some of the same creature comforts you may be used to back home. Coming to Cuba expecting the same luxuries as a five-star all-inclusive resort in Cancun may leave you disappointed.

Recommended Hotels

Havana	Trinidad
Hotel Saratoga	Hotel La Ronda
Hotel Iberostar Parque Central	Iberostar Grand Hotel Trinidad
Hotel Nacional de Cuba	**Varadero**
Viñales	Sol Palmeras
Rancho San Vicente	Paradisus Varadero Resort & Spa
Hotel Los Jazmines	Royalton Hicacos

Christine Williams & Julian Hatfield

Transport in Cuba

Everyone knows that old classic cars are one of the biggest attractions for tourists in Cuba. You'd struggle to find a magazine spread, online article, or travel blog that covers Cuba travel and doesn't reference this iconic part of the local culture. But old Chevys and Thunderbirds aren't the only timeless pieces of mobile history in Cuba. The country has an array of options for getting around at any budget.

Pedi-Cabs

A pedi-cab is as simple as it sounds: a little pedal-operated bicycle with a passenger seat at the back. You'll find them all throughout the country. They're a great option for both tourists and locals going short distances (but don't expect to pay the same price as the locals). Pedi-cabs can be a fun way to get around the city, giving you time to kick back and take in the views on your very own slow, personal tour. Don't be shy on haggling with the drivers. Remember that they're already charging you more than locals, especially if you look like a tourist.

Think of it this way. It might only cost $3-$4 for a 15-minute ride, but if you calculate that over an hour, it's more than $12. The pedi-cab drivers are already dominating the tourist transport industry, and the average Cuban doesn't make anywhere near that amount of cash in a day. Some Cubans struggle to make that in a week. It's not about being a scrooge: It's about making sure people are supported equally. Haggle about prices on the pedi-cab, take those savings, and then reinvest them in a local bar or restaurant. No one said you can't enjoy yourself while also spreading the wealth.

Classic Cars (The Old and the New)

When it comes to getting your taste of classic cars in Cuba, you have two options: the authentic, rickety budget option and the luxurious, more expensive tourist option. Needless to say, the luxury option is a nicer ride, but it'll also cost you a lot more cash, so your choice depends on your budget and your desired comfort level.

Luxury Car Rides

The luxury cars are the cream of the crop. They can be found in the big tourist cities, parked around the main town center waiting for tourists to pick them up. In Havana, there are three main places to grab a ride: around Parque Central, near the Plaza de Armas, or at La Feria. You won't have a hard time locating them and more than likely, they'll find you before you find them.

You rent the cars by the hour and prices can start as high as $40, with good negotiators being able to work down to $15 at the lowest. Generally speaking, the nicer or more classic the car, the more difficulty you'll have in negotiating a lower price. The way the drivers figure, there could always be another cashed-up tourist just around the corner ready to pay top dollar. And unfortunately for you, there usually always is.

The good thing about luxury car rentals is that you can fit up to four people in the car, so if you get it for $30, you pay only $7.50 each. That's still a bit of a stretch for Cuba prices, but much better than if you're just a couple. Even if you don't feel like spending the cash for a joyride, you can still take advantage of the amazing photo opp by posing in front of your favorite car. The drivers are usually fine with tourists grabbing a quick snap with their cars for free. They may hassle you to rent a car, or say that you can't take a photo, but a smile and a "Wow, what a beautiful car you have!" usually softens them up.

Budget Classic Cars

If you think $30 for an hour tour of the city is pricey, don't worry, there are alternatives. Luckily for you, Cuba's luxury car population is only a very small percentage of all the vintage cars cruising around the country. All over Cuban cities and towns, you'll find beat-up old versions of the classics. Although it might not be as nice as the luxury options, we like to think of these cars as having real...character. There's nothing like cramming into an old Chevy with faded paint, a busted-up fender, and a worn interior alongside six Cuban locals to give you an authentic experience. You can find old classic taxis or *colectivos* (shared taxis) cruising through the streets of any Cuban city. Most taxis will not have a meter, so be sure to agree on a price before entering the car. Locals generally pay between 10-15 CUP (40-60 cents) for a short ten-minute ride through Havana. Whichever option you choose, classic cars are definitely authentic Cuba. Even if you end up splurging with friends and renting one of the nicer options, you really should jump into one of the oldies to experience classic Cuba.

Viazul

For long-distance transportation, tourists only have a few options: either rent a car, fly (if you plan ahead, you can get a good deal), organize private transportation with a group, or take Viazul. Viazul is the tourist bus, Cuba's version of upscale transportation. But before you get too excited, realize that you're not going to be cruising around in a stretch limo. These buses are still cramped, uncomfortable, and *freezing*. For whatever reason, the drivers deem it necessary to blast the A/C, turning unprepared passengers into icicles. Definitely bring extra layers, especially on overnight journeys. ***Viazul*** (http://www.viazul.com/) has an official website where you can find all the routes, prices, and even book online ahead of time. If you're traveling in the high season, book as soon as you know your dates: The buses sell out.

Note: If you are at the bus station looking to move between cities, you can often get seats in shared taxis heading in the same direction as the bus for the same price or less. You'll need to be patient, and it's likely you'll have to haggle for the price, but it's a really fun way to travel.

Trains

On our most recent trip to Cuba, we had the opportunity to take a train across the country. Even after experiencing the old trucks, beaten-up cars, and freezing buses, train travel in Cuba is still on a different level. It's a lot of fun and another slice of authentic Cuba because you're almost guaranteed to be the only tourists on the train. It's not the most comfortable ride, and you won't get any sleep overnight, but it allows you to see a different side of Cuba. As the train chugs through the Cuban countryside, you'll marvel at how beautiful the interior of the country is.

The only thing to consider is that on the overnight train, you probably won't get much sleep. So if you're on a tight schedule or you need to factor in a big day of exploring after getting off the train, be aware you may be really tired. Besides, if you sleep on the train, you'll miss out on all the fun, like the guy who tries to sell you cheese and light bulbs...at the crack of dawn.

If a long train trip isn't your thing, consider taking the famous electric Hershey train. The Hershey train is reminiscent of an old subway car and travels between Matanzas and Old Havana, passing through the countryside of the Yumuri Valley.

Pro budget tip: If you're on a budget, taking the train across the country is a cheaper alternative to the Viazul tourist bus or flying. For example, a trip from Havana to Camaguey on Viazul would cost $33, whereas the train only costs $19. You'll also save money on accommodations by taking the overnight train. Double winning!

Other Budget Transportation Options

Aside from these transportation methods, there are a few other options that can shuttle you across the country on a dime. These are the super-budget options that the locals take, which are so cheap because they're subsidized by the government.

There is a lot of incorrect information in Cuba about whether tourists are allowed to take these types of transport. Most people within the tourism business will tell you the only option to get across the country is to fly or take the government-commissioned Viazul bus, which is a lot more expensive compared to local options. This isn't true. The only bus that you can't take is the Omnibus, which leaves from the same station as the Viazul. The Omnibus is a government-subsidized bus that requires you to have a local ID to board. But as far as the old converted dump trucks, *camionetas* (trucks), and *colectivo* buses (shared), you're good to go. The trucks and buses can often be found at the same bus station, or at least nearby. Cuba's transport network may be dated, but they successfully transport people all around the country everyday, so it works.

Authentic experience alert: Seeking out the local transport isn't just about the price: It truly is about the experience. Taking local transport is a perfect way to get a glimpse into the *real* Cuba. Even if you just try it once in your trip, it's totally worth it. You'll be squished in with locals and may have some little kid sitting on your knee, but it's such a unique way to see how Cuba operates outside of the tourist zone.

Budgeting for Cuba: From Low to High

When it comes to organizing a budget in Cuba, you have a lot of considerations to take into account. Obviously the first, and most determining, question is, "How much do you want to spend?" Cuba can be as expensive or cheap as you want it to be. The first time we traveled through the country in late-2013, we were spending less than $100 USD each a week for everything, but we were on a serious budget coming off two years of backpacking Latin America. In our more recent trip in mid-2016, we upped the budget to at least $200 USD each a week in order to make things a little easier and more enjoyable, but even that is still cheap compared to how most people travel in Cuba. Traveling in Cuba is rumored to be quite expensive, and like most countries, it can be if you follow the typical tourist routes. If you stay at high-end resorts, buy the best cigars, and get bottle-service at the clubs, it will be really pricey. Luckily, if you're on a budget, Cuba can be traveled on the cheap as well.

Whichever budget is more your style, it's important to know that there are basically two economies in Cuba: the local economy and the tourist economy (which is often represented through the dual currency system Cuba has). As you may have heard, locals don't make much money in Cuba. The most-quoted statistic is that a high-earning doctor makes around $40 USD per month, and that's really not far off the mark. Because Cubans aren't earning a lot of money, the government subsidizes a lot of the daily costs, which makes Cuba really cheap for the locals. Local transport and food cost almost nothing, and education and healthcare are free. This is one of few perks the Cuban people get out of Cuba's socialist economy. As a result of the subsidies, there are sometimes two different prices for locals and tourists, such as museum entrances and other attractions. Although it may seem frustrating having to pay more, it actually allows sights and museums to maintain their facilities while remaining accessible to locals who could never afford the tourist price.

If you want to stick to local food, accommodation, transportation, and so on, you can travel through Cuba on a tiny budget. Follow the path of the locals and Cuba is as cheap as it gets! On the other hand, if you stick to the tourist route, Cuba can be a bit pricey. High-end hotels, restaurants, and experiences cater to foreign tourists that come to Cuba with money. These can rack you up a pretty penny by the time you return home.

In this section, we detail three different budgets: budget travel, midrange, and high-end, with estimated prices for basic expenses. Prices listed will be in CUC/USD. As a general guideline, budget travel in Cuba should cost between $150-$250 a week, midrange travel will cost between $250-$500 a week, and high-end travel will cost more than $500.

Accommodation Costs

As always, accommodation is one of your biggest expenses while traveling. The same goes in Cuba, where you can spend as little or as much as your money permits.

Budget

Cuba doesn't have many budget options like you'd find in southeast Asia or Latin America, but as private business restrictions lessen, more people are embracing the hostel-type model. As more hostels pop up, offering dorm-style accommodation, you can find a bed in Havana for as little as $5-10 a night. If you're traveling as a couple, or with a friend, you can also find your own private room in a *casa particular* for as low as $15-20 if you know how to haggle. The bigger the group and the longer you stay, the more bargaining power you have to negotiate cheaper rates. Traveling as a group of four? Rent one room and ask for the second at 50 percent off—it's worth a shot.

Midrange

If you have a little more to spend, especially if you're traveling as a pair, you can find a more upscale *casa particular* for between $25-$40. This is not to say the rooms for $20 are crummy and rundown, but the difference between a $20 casa and a $40 casa is fairly significant. A $40 casa will generally include a breakfast, albeit a simple one, and the attention to detail will be a little higher. Nicer bedding, towels, location, and so on are a few of the perks of staying at a nicer casa. Most casas in the midrange mark should have extras like a fridge, A/C, and TV.

High-End

If you're not interested in staying in a family home, you can always book your own hotel room. Upscale hotels and resorts can start at $50 per night and go all the way up to the hundreds if you really want a high-end experience. For example, rooms at the Parque Central Hotel in the middle of Havana start at $300.

Drinking Costs

You can't visit Cuba without indulging in a couple of cocktails. And that doesn't mean you need to break the bank to do it. Here are a few examples of ways to enjoy your drinking in Cuba on different budgets.

Budget

Beers from the corner stores or local bars will cost between $1-$1.50, which often depends on how cold they are. Cristal is your standard beer recipe that you'll find around the world. Bucanero is referred to as *fuerte* (strong), but just has a little fuller taste. Both get the job done on a hot Caribbean afternoon. Decent bottles of

Havana Club rum start at $3.50 for 700 ml and it really wouldn't be worth getting anything cheaper than that. It's legal to drink on the street in Cuba, so feel free to grab a bottle from the store and enjoy it in a plaza. It's a cheap way to have a drink and get involved with the locals who will be out there with you.

Midrange

You can find affordable cocktails at bars and lounges for $2-5. These are usually limited to simple drinks, including local favorites like *Cuba Libres* (rum, Coke, and lime) and mojitos. You're likely to find some live music in these types of bars, depending on the time of day and how busy it is. If you're after a fancier beer experience, you can try some of the craft beer spots that are popping up around Havana. We mention more about that later on in the **'Must-See Experiences'** chapter.

High-End

Cocktails at fancier bars and restaurants will be a bit pricier at $5 and up, but are often still quite affordable. You'll find yourself paying more for the atmosphere than the quality of drinks, especially at tourist favorites like Hemingway's old stomping ground, El Floridita. The Hotel Nacional de Cuba, which overlooks the beach, is a popular spot for sunset cocktails and is a pleasant spot to enjoy the afternoon.

Food Costs

Small street-side stalls, locally ran eateries or fancy sit down restaurants, Cuba has it all when it comes to food. It varies in quality, but there's always something no matter what your budget.

Budget

Street food in Cuba is cheap, dirt cheap. You can eat meals for 25-50 cents. It may not be the best food, but it gets the job done and it's definitely worth experiencing at least once. If you find the privately-run paladares, the meals for 80c-$1 are decent and you could easily live off them for a couple of weeks.

Midrange

There are plenty of midrange restaurants if you're looking to spend $5-10 on a meal. This usually consists of meat or fish, rice and beans, a small salad, and maybe plantain chips. At the *casa particulares,* you can eat home-cooked meals for $2-5, generally. The midrange restaurants are usually the government or private places you find in tourist areas. To be honest, we've had meals in the $5-6 range that don't taste much different than a $1 paladar meal, but you're paying for a marginally improved atmosphere. Midrange restaurants will have nicer seating and ambience, and are likely to have nice music or salsa dancing while you eat.

High-End

You can find high-end restaurants, mostly in Havana and other big cities, where meals will cost $15 and up. At these locations, you'll be paying for the ambience as much as the food, if not more. The benefit of high-end restaurants is you'll usually get some nice music at the venue, but don't expect it to be included in the price. You'll still be expected to tip!

Entertainment Costs

Flashy cabaret shows, nights of salsa dancing or waterfront guitar shows. There's plenty of entertainment on offer in Cuba!

Budget

As cheesy as it sounds, there is plenty of entertainment for free, right at your doorstep in Cuba. From domino games on the corner to bands playing in the street, you really don't need to purchase tickets to anything to feel entertained. As most Cubans can't afford the high prices of bars and clubs, they have learned to become pretty resourceful over the years. Follow the locals on a Friday or Saturday night down to the Malecon (a waterfront spot popular with locals discussed in **Must-See Experiences**) and you'll find some fun. For the price of a couple cocktails, you can also find some very talented musicians playing in the local bars.

Midrange

Although a bit touristy, Casa de Musica is a must-do in Cuba for a night of drinks and dancing. The entrance costs around $10. Other bars or clubs charge a similar fee, some including a free drink. Bring your dancing shoes and brush up on your salsa because you're likely to be dancing the night away.

High-End

Cabaret shows are a quite-popular event in Havana, but they're not cheap. One of the most famous, the Cabaret Tropicana, will cost you upwards of $75 for tickets. Compared to seeing a show on the West End in London, for example, this is pretty on-par for a high quality show around the world. But to put this in perspective, we traveled through Cuba in 2013 spending about $100 each for a week, so for Cuba's standards, it's expensive. Still, the cabarets and other shows have reputations for being grandiose productions and it could be a once-in-a-lifetime experience. As much as you can find free entertainment in the city, you'll never find something as spectacular as the Cabaret Tropicana in the backstreets of Havana.

Sightseeing Costs

Walk the streets for free, exploring the historical sites and revolution memorials. Hit the museums and tours that show you the deeper side of Cuba, or get your dose of adventure with the many activities on offer.

Budget

There are several free attractions in any city you visit. These might include monuments to the revolution, parks, and other public spaces. From there, it's up to you what attractions you'd like to splurge on. Paying $8 at the *Museo de la Revolución* may feel like quite a bit when your daily budget is $15, but we recommend stretching your budget for these iconic attractions. When you return home and pay $8 for a craft beer, you'll regret not spending that money on your trip.

Midrange

There are plenty of midrange activities and sightseeing opportunities throughout the country. Most of the historical museums cost between $5-10, and you can usually add on a guide for a couple of extra dollars if you're interested. Activities like snorkeling, caving, or trekking with a guide will cost between $10-20.

High-End

More expensive activities include scuba diving, which costs around $30 or more per dive, and full day tours with a guide. You can hire a driver for an hour in Havana and cruise in one of the gorgeous classic cars for between $25-$35.

Transportation Costs

There's something for everyone's level of comfort when it comes to transportation. Rough it with the cheaper options, or pay to have a little extra plush as you make it around Cuba.

Budget

Local transportation is by far the cheapest option. City buses cost 0.4 CUP (1 cent). *Colectivos* (shared taxis) are also a great budget option. These can be quite economical for inner-city travel, although a bit difficult to distinguish from normal private taxis. Always agree on a price with the driver *before* getting in. Taking public transportation between cities will cost a couple of dollars, although it won't be comfortable.

Midrange

Viazul is the fairly comfortable air-conditioned tourist bus that costs around $3-$4 per hour. This is the easiest way to travel long distances. Here you'll get your own seat and a relatively comfortable ride in comparison to the train or local buses. Unless you're on a really tight budget, Viazul is the most convenient and cost-effective way to get around. You'll find all types of travelers on a Viazul bus, so it might even be an opportunity to meet another traveler if you're solo.

High-end

For getting around the city, especially if you're traveling with a few people, you can rent your own car for $50 or more a day. It's possible to arrange this when you arrive in Cuba, and it's likely your host or hotel will know someone that can help you out. If you find something online, it's always going to cost you more, but you have the benefit of securing a booking. Renting a car allows you to visit those out-of-town places all in a day, with the convenience of stopping whenever you want. But remember, Cuba is a place to be experienced and not just seen. If you hire a car just to cruise by a million places, chances are, you won't have any time to actually experience them. If your group has more than four people and you need to get around, we recommend hiring private transportation.

Christine Williams & Julian Hatfield

Safety in Cuba

Cuba is incredibly safe for tourists. In fact, over the last seven years of travel, it has been one of the safest countries we've visited. Like all information in this book, our opinion on safety is a reflection of our own personal experience in Cuba. We can't guarantee your safety and it's always important to acknowledge your surroundings and exercise a degree of caution when at home or abroad.

So How Safe Is Cuba?

Cuba is "arriving from the airport at 1 a.m., walking around the streets of Havana trying to find our accommodation and ending up in a random family's house drinking coffee" safe. Cuba is "coming home from a bar at 2 a.m. with our DSLR cameras around our necks, walking down the backstreets past groups of adolescent boys, and saying '*hola, amigos*'" safe. Honestly, we've never felt safer than our times traveling through Cuba. The people are incredibly hospitable and the worst you'll likely experience is a few scammers (see chapter **Avoiding Scams**).

Whether you're walking the streets with a camera, leaving your possessions in a *casa particular,* or jumping into a local taxi, you can feel at ease in Cuba as a tourist. Like many other places around the world, you should exercise a normal degree of awareness when out in public places, but you shouldn't feel threatened or nervous to travel to Cuba, whether you're a group of older travelers or a solo female backpacker. Any crime that could occur will most likely be opportunistic, such as pickpocketing, or overcharging you on a taxi, and not threatening.

Simple common sense is the best preventative for being a target of petty theft or the like. It's really no different then what you would do while traveling in your own home city. Don't withdraw and flash around wads of cash at the ATM. You're most likely not going to get robbed in the middle of Havana, but you also don't need to advertise that you're a walking cash machine. Don't leave your camera unattended on the table while going to the bathroom. Chances are, it'll be there when you get back, but when your camera is the equivalent of a yearly Cuban wage, you don't want to take a risk.

Be aware of pickpockets in the bigger cities and places like nightclubs or bustling salsa bars. Calle Obispo is the main pedestrian walking street in Old Havana and can get very crowded in the high season. Although it's well policed with both officers and cameras, pickpockets thrive in this kind of setting. With more tourists coming to Cuba every month, there are growing reports of wallets magically disappearing from crowded areas. There are also a few incidences of crafty (and beautiful) females preying on unsuspecting men during flirty dance encounters out at bars or clubs. One moment you're a Casanova as that twenty-something girl teaches you a few new salsa moves; the next, you're walking home because you've "lost" your wallet. By no means is this guaranteed to happen, but it is something to be conscious of. And ladies, don't think you're immune to this either. You'll see your fair share of toned and tanned Latin guys carving up the dance floor. Be mindful when they start to get handsy, it mightn't be just your booty they're after. Men, for more on protecting yourself from Cuba's beauties, check out **Traveling as a Solo Male**.

Why Is Cuba So Safe?

Why is Cuba largely free of violent crime? To put it bluntly, Cubans are pretty terrified of the government. While this terror has many negative aspects for the Cuban people, as a tourist, it works relatively well in keeping you safe. For the people of Cuba, there are harsh punishments for breaking the law, especially committing crimes against tourists. The police state that the Cuban government has created comes back to the fact that Cuba is a socialist country. Part of being a communist or socialist government is ensuring complete control over your citizens, making sure there is no room for anti-government pushback. In order to maintain this control, Cuba has created strong laws and punishments against guns, gangs, drugs, violence, and anything else that would threaten their power and control. It also means that over the last seventy-odd years, since the Communist Party of Cuba took control of the government, this nonviolent mentality has become imbedded in the

Cuban culture. Decades of nonviolence has had a significant effect on the people of Cuba, where disputes are handled more casually and where most people go about their own business without hassling others.

Add tourists into the equation, especially considering that tourism is one of Cuba's main exports, and the government is extra careful about protecting its most important asset…you! Protecting the tourists (and the tourism money) is of utmost importance to the government. According to a 2015 report from the World Travel and Tourism Council, tourism makes up more than 11 percent of Cuba's GDP, a number that is set to rise over the next decade. Tourism also accounts for more than 10 percent of all employment in Cuba, another figure set to rise significantly in the next ten years. Additionally, almost 17 percent of all exports come from visitors to the country, so Cuba's economy really relies on increased tourism to the country.

With economic interests in mind, Cuba works hard to protect its visitors. In some cases, Cubans aren't even allowed to talk to tourists unless they have a valid reason to do so, such as workers in hospitality, retail, or food service, and so on. If the average Cuban decides to stop you on the street for a chat, police might shuffle them on if it looks suspicious. One night while walking down the Malecon (a popular place for locals to hang out), the police took down the information of all our new Cuban amigos just because they were chatting with us. Even after we assured the police that we were simply chatting and hanging out, the police erred on the side of caution and recorded everyone's details. When we asked why the police hassled them, they indicated that technically they should be leaving us alone.

In another example, we saw the police question a Cuban guy on the street and take him away for further questioning at the station. He had been hanging around some tourists near Plaza de Armas in Havana when the police officers escorted him away. When we saw the same guy a few hours later, we asked him about it. He told us that the authorities saw him on the cameras talking to tourists (yes, Cuba has lots of public surveillance) and they wanted to know why.

This doesn't mean you should be dissuaded from making local friends, but just be aware the government is probably keeping an eye on you, whether you know it or not.

Traveling as a Solo Female

Traveling the world as a solo female is an awesome, empowering experience, but it also comes with a lot of issues that guys don't have to deal with while traveling, such as the constant persistence of male attention and having to carefully execute your schedule so you're not stuck walking home alone in the dark. There are very few places in the world where females don't have to be hyperaware of their surroundings to stay safe. As a solo female traveler for many years, Christine can attest to that, but as far as Cuba goes, we've always traveled as a couple. Therefore, we reached out to a travel writer buddy of ours who recently visited Cuba in October 2016 to help recall what it is like for solo female travelers in Cuba.

The following information comes from the travel writer and blogger Claire Sturzaker at Tales of a Backpacker. You can follow her adventures on her blog: **http://talesofabackpacker.com/**

Safety as a Solo Female

Relatively speaking, Cuba is a very safe country for solo females. Violent crime is rare, so wandering around the streets at night is pretty safe. I never say never, so it's important to still be aware of your surroundings and not take unnecessary risks, but unlike other

Latin American countries, Cuba is generally safe to walk around alone at night, even for a woman.

Unfortunately, like most other Latin American countries, catcalling, kissy noises, and various lewd comments are frustratingly common. It's practically impossible to walk for 50 meters by yourself without encountering some sort interaction and attention. As annoying as this is (and it does get very wearing very quickly), that is all it will be.

Be wary of taking tours alone, or be sure to book your tours with official organizations. I had an "enthusiastic" unofficial guide in Viñales who was decidedly over-friendly. Luckily there was another girl with me at the time, so I didn't feel in danger. He had invited his friend along to accompany her, and I overheard them decide which one of them would go for which one of us, so I knew what was coming and was prepared. A firm "no" usually does the trick, no matter how insistent they are.

Solo Female Scams

The good thing is that usually, the only real way that men will take advantage of you is to scam you out of a few dollars. In general, the people are really friendly. Perhaps you won't mind being scammed, as long as it's not for too much money, but I hate being lied to. On the one hand, you have to admire their ingenuity, but it's still dishonest and hard not to feel like you've been had.

Even with your guard up, it is difficult to resist the handsome Cubanos who approach foreigners and strike up a conversation, perhaps asking you to take a photo of them, or offering to take you to their favorite place. If someone offers to take you somewhere, check how much it is before you agree, and how much the drinks will be if it is a bar. Three dollars for a mojito is a fair price in most bars. Any more than that is probably a scam, unless you're in a bar like El Floridita, which is famous and expensive. Any event or attraction where locals go will be maximum of $1 CUC entrance fee, around 25 pesos *nacionales*, so if someone offers to take you somewhere, and asks for some cash to pay on your behalf, don't give them more than a couple of CUC.

After traveling in South America for nearly a year, I thought I was prepared for anything that I would encounter in Cuba, but even experienced travelers like me get hoodwinked every now and again. In fact, almost every solo woman I spoke to had fallen for some trick like this, even the most careful ones! For more information about scams, read my personal experience in **Avoiding Scams.**

I found Havana exhausting because I had to be constantly on my guard, knowing that many people striking up a conversation would be out to scam a few bucks out of me. That isn't to say you should ignore every conversation. After I left Havana, my new travel buddy and I met plenty more people—both foreign and Cuban— who were more genuine and great fun. We found the smaller cities and towns less stressful and we felt less subjected to scams than in Havana.

The best advice I can give is to be prepared. Be prepared for a lot of male attention, be prepared for feeling like a walking ATM, but also be prepared to look beyond that. Cuba is a beautiful country, and many people there are desperate—they are not bad people, but they assume that any tourist going to Cuba has a lot of money, and they just want to make a living. If you do anything with local people, you will probably be expected to pay for it, from a casual drink, a taxi, or a meal.

Find a Travel Buddy

Finding a travel buddy is a good way to feel safer as a solo female and save money: Sharing a twin or double room halves your accommodation costs. Some casas have three beds in their rooms, or perhaps a double and a single bed, meaning up to three people can share one room and split the price. Usually the casa owners are more than happy for you to share as more people in the room means more breakfasts and other extras than a solo traveler would use.

However, it can be tough to find buddies without the hostel social areas you may be used to. If you start your trip in Havana, I highly recommend staying at a hostel where you can meet other travelers (see our list of recommended hostels in our Accommodation Costs section). I stayed in Casa Magnolia, also known as Hostel Hamel, and met a network of travelers and casa owners who Magnolia calls to arrange shared rooms in the hostels. Another good alternative is Hostel Casa Caribe, where I met a Spanish girl who became my travel buddy. We traveled together for around ten days.

Couchsurfing is still rare due mainly to lack of W-Fi and gray-area legalities, but in Havana, there are regular meet-ups arranged by Casa Tacos, a tiny restaurant and bar in Centro Havana. They usually have events on a Tuesday that attract mainly foreigners, but some Cubans too. You can chat and get to know people, relatively safe in the knowledge they aren't out to rip you off.

Be Flexible

If you want to find people to travel with, be flexible. I recommend booking your first couple of nights in Havana before you arrive in Cuba. After that, you can have a rough itinerary, but be open to changing your plans if you want to travel with other people. If you already have everything confirmed, you have less chance of finding someone doing exactly the same trip as you, and you will end up paying more money for rooms by yourself. I usually preferred to ask my casa to call ahead to my next destination to arrange a room for me. That way, when I got off the bus, I wouldn't have to fight through the group of people offering me cheap rooms and I would know exactly where I was going. Alternatively, you could see who else is traveling on your bus or *colectivo* and see if you can arrange to share a room with them. Other solo travelers are usually open to meeting new people, sharing rooms, and cutting costs, just like you!

Luckily Cuba is one place where a female should feel 100 percent comfortable traveling solo. As in any country, you should use common sense, but Cuba is generally very safe. As we've explained, there are very strict laws protecting tourists so you can almost guarantee you won't have any physical confrontations. There is always a risk of theft or pickpocketing, but the chance of being met with a violent attack is very low. In the 1950s, Castro recalled guns from the general public, so gun ownership is low to nonexistent. Still, there are a few things to be aware of as a woman.

Traveling as a Solo Male

When you think of independent travel, you might not always think a lot of safety precautions are needed for men traveling solo. And although it might be true in some aspects, being a solo male traveler opens you up to a whole range of other difficulties and potential problems.

The Cuban Ladies

Cuban women are gorgeous, sassy, and independent, and some of them want more than just your company for the night. As a solo male traveler, particularly if you're younger than forty, you can expect to find a bit of attention from a few of these ladies if you hang around the bars or touristy spots at night.

People joke that the only true form of capitalism that exists in Cuba is prostitution. And in many ways, they're not wrong. While the government can police it, they can't exactly control or tax a woman's ability to sell her body. As a result, independent women set their own hours, prices, and can provide themselves with a genuine opportunity to better their lives. When a working girl can make the equivalent of one months' wage in one night, you can't really blame them for taking advantage of the situation.

Beautiful Cuban women have been working their magic on tourists for years. You can find them in the bars or just about anywhere tourists hang out at night. They'll invigorate the Latin lover in anyone, but only for a fee. And while there's no denying that Cuba has a number of prostitutes, not all women are prowling the streets looking for that lucky someone. Some women may just try their luck with foreigners, opportunistically, to see if they can get a few free drinks out of it. If they're already attracted to you, and can work out a night of fine dining and fun, why not give it a shot? A woman doesn't necessarily want to sleep with you just because she asked you to buy her a drink in a bar.

And just to clarify, we're not saying that every Cuban woman you meet as a single male is trying to work you. It would be terrible to think people are visiting Cuba and assuming every woman is on the clock. Cuban women are friendly, flirty, and the majority of them aren't interested in you or your money. All we're saying is be aware. If you get extra special attention, there could be a catch.

Offers to Buy Drugs

Needless to say, buying drugs in Cuba isn't a very smart idea! As a male, you're probably more likely than a female to be approached by people in the street offering to sell you cocaine or weed, but it's not a proposition you should entertain.

For the buyer (or silly tourist), there are numerous stories of police going undercover as drug dealers trying to catch foreigners. Forget what you know about entrapment: That's not going to hold up in Cuba. And while it's unlikely you'll face a big jail sentence (it depends how much you're buying), you could be hit with a big fine, deported, and never be allowed back in. Either that, or you'll have to pay an "on the spot" fine, which is more than likely a bribe.

Despite Cuba's declarations that drugs aren't a problem, there are recent news reports that suggest drugs are becoming a growing concern for the government and community. In 2013, I don't recall ever being asked if I wanted to buy cocaine, but on our most recent trip in 2016, I was asked a couple of times at night around the Parque Central area. It's a big gamble for the buyer because, if caught, dealers can face up to thirty years or possibly life in jail.

Christine Williams & Julian Hatfield

Traveling as a Couple

Cuba is a wonderful country to travel as a couple. It's romantic and memorable and traveling as a pair means you can split a lot of the costs along the way. There isn't really anything different to note between traveling as a couple or traveling with a group of friends. Rooms in *casa particulares* may have one double bed or two twins, but you can usually request one or the other. Unmarried couples shouldn't have any problems renting a room. You may have the occasional casa owner (generally the older generation) ask if you're married. You don't have to say yes, but remember that Cuba is a predominantly Catholic country and some people are still pretty conservative. Saying yes doesn't mean you have to tell a big lie to them, but it might make them feel more comfortable.

When traveling through the country, don't be nervous to split up for the day and do your own thing. Cuba is an extremely safe country to travel as a solo male or female, so feel free to go on your own solo adventure.

Note on Dress Code for all Travelers

We're big believers in matching your modesty level of dress to the customs of the locals, especially after seeing so many male backpackers with their tops off and females in booty shorts in conservative communities. But in Cuba, you'll probably end up feeling like the modest one. We'll just say the woman dress "freely." Tight and short is the best description. From the minute you step off the airplane, you'll see female airport security guards in tight skirts, fishnet stockings and heels. Of course, not all Cuban woman dress like this, but it's not frowned-upon either. Feel free to wear what you want in Cuba.

Christine Williams & Julian Hatfield

Avoiding Scams

Although it's true that Cuba has a few scam artists working the streets, one thing that you can be sure of is your safety. They might try to skim a little off the top, take you for a ride, or blatantly cheat you, but they're never going to endanger your safety. What you'll find in Cuba are opportunistic people who have creatively derived a couple of scams to earn a few extra bucks. Remember, the monthly wage in Cuba can be as low as $25-$30 dollars, so even if they could scam a few dollars off of a tourist every day, they'd be making more than at a government-sanctioned job. Some of the scams in Cuba are pretty obvious, but others not so much. Some are actually quite creative and you have to admire their ability to think outside the box. Cubans have definitely been making lemonade with their lemons.

Knowing and avoiding the scams isn't as much about denying the average Cuban a little extra living: It's more about the principle of being scammed. Some Cubans are actually making a decent living off the tourist scams and that doesn't really sit right with us. We'd much prefer to have our money going towards honest people, and if you would too, here are a couple of Cuban scams to avoid.

Buying Fake Cigars

By far, the most common scam in Cuba for tourists is getting ripped off on fake cigars. You can't walk down a tourist street in Havana without someone popping their head out of a shop or house asking you to buy "original" Montecristos. What they'll most likely be selling you are the cheapest cigars in all of Cuba, which you can buy for 1 Cuban peso (5 cents) in any local store. These cheap cigars have nothing in common with the originals, except the expensive price tag from the hagglers trying to hawk them to you. If you're even more unlucky, you'll get one layer of tobacco leaf for the smell, and the rest dried banana tree leaves.

If you're looking to buy singles or boxes of authentic Cuban cigars, you have to stick to the government-run shops. The Casa del Habano and Caracol shops are the official businesses and sell all the original cigars and rum. You'll find them in all the major tourists spots and you can buy from them with confidence that you're getting the real thing.

Warning: Some of the fake cigar scammers are even cheeky enough to stand outside the official government store to try and sell you their "cigars." They're not aggressive in their sale. Just decline, no matter how persuasive they seem. When they offer you a significantly cheaper price, just give them a wink and say you're not looking for fake cigars.

Christine Williams & Julian Hatfield

Salsa Festival/Buena Vista Social Club

Scammers are kind of like sharks: They can smell fresh, unknowing tourists from a mile away. Even before you notice them eyeing you off, they'll see you walking down the street, camera and map in hand with an eager smile on your face. In an instant, they'll weigh you up, studying your age, gender, potential country of origin, and all the other things that will be best applicable to their scam. It's all these factors that come into play with this next scam that is one of the most common in the busy streets of Havana.

The basic premise behind this scam can come in a couple of different versions, but the outcome is always the same. While walking through the streets, a very unsuspicious and charming local (usually a man or couple) will come up to you and strike up a conversation. After some general chatter, they'll try to convince you to accompany them to a local salsa festival or to the "real" Buena Vista Social Club. Unfortunately, instead of going to where they suggested, they'll take you to their friend's bar where they work for commissions. You'll buy a couple of drinks, or at least be convinced to do so. Your new friends will then make you feel obliged to buy them drinks. Heck, they'll even be super friendly about it, but secretly they're taking a cut from the owner under the table. Because they've brought you to the bar, they'll get a "referral fee" on whatever you spend, so they'll be hoping you spend a bit. And what's worse is that often the drinks you purchase for them won't be alcoholic, even though you're paying full price for them.

By the end of the session, you'll be buying overpriced drinks, and guess who gets to pay the overpriced bill when everything wraps up?

Scammers in Action

As told by Claire Sturzaker from Tales of a Backpacker

While in Havana, I was approached by a charming, cute Cuban guy who asked me to take a photo of him, which was a nice, casual introduction and different to the usual, "Hey, lady, where are you from?" that most scammers use. He offered to take me to a train carriage that was used by royalty, which was free to enter, so I figured what the hell. I wanted to meet the locals, after all. Then when he offered to take me to the Jesus statue on the other side of the bay by boat, I agreed—I wanted to go! But when he asked me for 5 CUC for the ferry crossing, I was immediately suspicious. I was the only tourist on the boat, and for sure the price was no more than 1 CUC, even for gringos like me. I was annoyed, but he was so sweet and polite, I let it slide. However, when we went for a drink later and had already ordered he explained he didn't have any money in CUC, so I got stuck with the bill for four mojitos costing $16 CUC. It could have been worse: A friend of mine got stung for two mojitos for $18 CUC, so I guess I got off lightly!

The City Is Closed

Generally, the "city is closed" scam occurs when you're walking through Havana, most likely on the outskirts of the main tourist areas. You'll stop at a traffic light, or to look at an attraction, and a male/female couple will approach you. They generally work in a couple to make it seem like they're a little more approachable, but they could also be solo.

The couple will chat to you about the city and act friendly (remember, they're not malicious people), striking up a conversation about your travels. They'll ask where you're going, what you want to see, and before you know it, they'll launch into a little bit of a spiel explaining that the city center is closed that day. They'll make up a story about there being a political event or the city being fumigated, and then offer to take you to another location that is open. While it's true that Cuba takes fumigation pretty seriously, they're definitely not about to close the city for it. Like the Buena Vista Social Club or Salsa Festival scam, you'll be led to their friend's bar or restaurant where they work for commission. Friendly conversation will follow with drinks or food, and the rest is history. If you're extra-lucky, they'll even try to combine scams and sell you some knock-off cigars. Don't be a sucker! If a Cuban approaches you in the street, you don't need to immediately distrust them, but if they start to try convince you about festivals, closures, and such, you should be wary.

Milk Powder or Other Baby Products

The milk powder scam is a bit of a tearjerker, but you've got to be strong. It is a scam. Mothers with young kids will come up to you in the street asking if you can help buy milk or food for their starving young children. As you can imagine, it can be quite difficult to turn your back and say no to them, but believe us: It's a scam. This is what will happen. A mother will approach you begging for help. They'll pick you from within the crowd and appeal to your good nature. She'll come up to you with her kid, pleading with you to help her, that her child has no food or that they're sick. If you willingly oblige, you'll end up being taken to a store to buy milk powder or some other food product in bulk, probably about $20 worth.

You'll walk away feeling good about yourself, but that same lady will go back to the store, put all the products back on the shelf, and split the commissions with the shopkeeper. Trust us: It happens. We know some really good people who fell for this, unfortunately. But how do you know this is a scam and not just someone in need? Great question. In Cuba, although the people might not have a lot of financial opportunity, they do have incredible free healthcare, especially for infants and youth. Cuban mothers who are expecting a child will receive extra rations to make sure they are nourished. Once they've given birth, the mothers continue to receive extra food, have free, regular check-ups, and the utmost attention paid to their child's health. In Cuba, the infant mortality rate is lower than in the US. Trust us: They look after their kids.

Begging

In Cuba, a lot of people have taken to the streets to beg even though they don't need to. Although it's no secret that some Cubans are living in poverty, their poverty rate is extremely low: less than 2 percent of the population (according to government stats). That's not to say that Cubans aren't poor, but they do receive free education, free healthcare, subsidized food, and assistance with many other public services. As a nation, impoverished Cubans get looked after better than many disadvantaged citizens from the western world, especially compared to poorer citizens in the developing world. And if they want to work, the government will find them a job.

An example of this comes from a beggar we met in Camaguey. He came into a restaurant where we were eating. He asked for money, and the manager kicked him out and apologized to us. We assured him we didn't mind, but used this as an opportunity to ask him about the beggar situation in Cuba. He told us he had known this man a long time. The man from the street had, more or less, always been a drunk. A few weeks ago, he had helped him clean up his act and get a job with the government as a pedi-cab driver. After weeks of working, the man realized he could make more money begging and he had already quit and gone back to the streets to beg for money and buy booze. In Cuba, if you want to work, there is a job for you, the manager told us.

Other Scams

Not really a scam, but more locals taking advantage of the tourists, will be the extreme price rises you find in tourist areas. Be prepared to haggle in Cuba to get a fair price. Don't be shy, either: It's actually a part of the culture to negotiate on prices. I know it seems weird to walk into a store and start negotiating prices, even with items that have a price tag, but it's expected. If you don't, you'll be straight-up ripped off! For more information on haggling, check out our **Cuba Travel Hacks** section.

Christine Williams & Julian Hatfield

Getting Sick in Cuba

Any time you travel abroad, it's important to be aware of the health issues of the country you're visiting. In Cuba, there is a relatively low risk of getting seriously sick if you protect yourself with the right vaccines. The following table is a list of the most common diseases, viruses, and recommended vaccines in Cuba. This is information from the US Centers for Disease Control and Prevention (CDC), as well as other travel medical recommendations. Please use this list only as a guide and always seek professional medical advice before planning your next trip.

Recommend and Required Vaccines and Medication

Malaria	There is no vaccine for malaria, only medication that you can take to prevent contracting the disease. The CDC notes that malaria is not a problem in Cuba and there are no recommendations to carry malarial medication.

Dengue	Dengue fever is the most common mosquito-borne disease, but even still, the chances of contracting it are extremely low. There is no vaccine for dengue fever, nor is there any preventative medication, so the best advice is to cover up and wear a good mosquito repellant. Cases are rare, but they do occur (as you'll read more about later in this section).
Zika	In October 2016, the CDC upgraded the Zika virus threat to level 2, which means to exercise enhanced precautions. Unfortunately, no vaccine is available, so, as with dengue, the best method of prevention is to avoid contact with Zika-carrying mosquitoes. Overall, the reported cases and chances of contracting is are very low and shouldn't deter you from traveling to Cuba.
Hepatitis A	This is a recommended vaccination if you're traveling to Cuba. A lot of people may have already received Hepatitis A vaccinations in school or from previous trips, but if you haven't, get one: It's a simple shot. If you have had the shot before, you might require a booster, so speak to your doctor.

Typhoid	Typhoid is a nasty food- and waterborne disease that you can be vaccinated against. It's recommended for Cuba or whenever you leave the country.
Rabies	Rabies is not a common viral disease in Cuba and it is not a recommended vaccination unless you know you're going to be in areas with lots of animals, or in Cuba for an extended period of time. We have never had rabies shots before and have not heard of them as necessary for Cuba.
Yellow Fever	You can receive a yellow fever vaccination, but it is not required for Cuba and does not present itself as a concern according to the CDC.
Tetanus	Most people have been vaccinated for tetanus. We recommend this vaccination, and if you already have it, you should check whether you need a booster.

Aside from the previously mentioned diseases and viruses, you're more likely, if anything, to pick up a bit of a stomach bug that is very hard to avoid or prevent. Stomach bugs aren't usually much to worry about and, at you'll generally shake it within twenty-four hours. If you're feeling a bit worse for the wear, you can get basic painkillers or flu medication from local pharmacy stores. If you feel particularly bad, or it lasts longer than a couple of days, we recommend going to the hospital to get checked out. It's difficult to distinguish between a twenty-four-hour stomach bug and something more serious like a parasite, but after a couple of days, it's likely you'll need some more serious medication. Luckily, if you do get sick, Cuba has a very reliable healthcare system. The doctors are excellent and they have everything you need in terms of equipment and facilities. Cuba is famous for their expert doctors, and many of them travel around the world providing world-class service to developing communities and disaster zones.

Regarding Cuban healthcare, we can speak from first-hand experience because Christine picked up dengue fever in Havana during our last trip. Originally, Christine experienced flu-like symptoms. After a couple of days of exhaustion and bedrest, she finally went to the clinic for a check-up. The doctors at the international hospital ran tests, gave her a hydration IV, and sent her in the ambulance to the tropical diseases hospital for further tests. She ended up spending the next four nights in the Pedro Kouri Institute of Tropical Diseases (twenty-five minutes outside of central Havana) Although the experience was obviously unpleasant, the majority of the hospital staff were friendly and helpful.

> **Note:** If you're traveling solo and have to go a clinic, carry a business card from the hotel or *casa particular* that you are staying at so you can contact them if you need to be kept overnight. When Christine checked herself into the clinic, we had no idea we'd end up at the tropical diseases hospital for four days, so I had to go back into Havana to let our host know we'd need a few extra days.

Overall there isn't a great concern for illness in Cuba, and there's a good chance that Christine's dengue was actually contracted in Mexico before we even arrived in Havana. However, we can't stress enough how important it is to get travel insurance. Technically, it's mandatory for all travelers to Cuba, and the Cuban officials at the airport may force you to buy the national insurance if you don't have proof you're already insured. We weren't prompted to show our documents, nor have we heard of other people, but regardless, travel insurance is important to have any time you travel. While Cuba may be the land of free healthcare for its citizens, it's not that cheap if you're a foreigner. For the four nights Christine was in the hospital, she racked up an $800 USD bill. Thank goodness Christine had travel insurance and received all her money back!

Note: If you take prescription medications, make sure to bring enough with you to cover your whole trip. You may be able to find what you need in an emergency, but we definitely wouldn't chance it. We didn't see any pharmacies stocking much more than paracetamol and cold medication during our trip.

Christine Williams & Julian Hatfield

How to Find Internet in Cuba

Gone are the days when Internet in Cuba was nonexistent and you could really disconnect yourself from the world. Now, more than ever, it's easier to connect to the Internet in Cuba. And unsurprisingly, considering how long it has taken Cuba to get online, many people are jumping at the opportunity to connect with the rest of the world.

As a tourist, this makes traveling in Cuba that little bit more manageable and accessible. You can now do more research while in Cuba, check back in with any work you might have on the go, and post social media updates to make all your friends back home jealous. Sure, you still have to wait in line for half an hour in Havana to buy an Internet card and then find a Wi-Fi spot, but at $2 an hour, it's much better than it was back in 2013 when Internet was $6-8 an hour and you were constrained to the slow desktop computers in the government-designated Internet cafes.

There are four main ways to get online in Cuba, each with its own set of conveniences and setbacks. We'll walk you through each of the ways and you can work out which is the best for you based on time, budget, and convenience.

Buy an Internet Card at an ETECSA Store

We think the cheapest and most efficient way to get online in Cuba is to visit the official government telecommunications store, ETECSA, and buy a Wi-Fi card. You can purchase up to three cards per person. There are one-hour cards for $2, or you can buy a five-hour card for $10. There is no economic advantage between the two, but you will be able to buy up to three five-hour cards (fifteen hours in total) per person if you need Internet and want to stock up.

In Havana, on the main tourist street of Calle Obispo, you may wait in line for half an hour to get into the store and get served, but if you're buying a few cards, it's well worth the wait. In other cities around Cuba, the wait isn't as long and you can get in the store within a few minutes, depending on the time of day. After you've purchased your Internet card, it's as simple as finding one of the Wi-Fi locations scattered throughout the city, logging into your device, and then making sure you log off when you're finished with your session (to ensure your Internet time doesn't keep ticking over). The Internet speed isn't great, as you might expect, but it's manageable if you need to check emails, do research, and get onto Facebook.

Pro Tip: Bring some form of identification to the store to verify the purchase. They won't always ask you for it, but have it just in case. It doesn't have to be a passport: Even your driver's license will do.

Buying Internet from a Hotel

At most of the major hotels, you can find a Wi-Fi connection, and you can log in using the same ETECSA cards. The hotels also have the added benefit of a nice comfortable air-conditioned lobby that you can lounge in. However, if you need to buy an ETECSA card for the hotels, you may pay upwards of $4-5 dollars for the same card you can buy for $2 in an ETECSA store. Unless you're desperate, don't choose this option.

Pro Tip: Buy your cards at the official ETECSA store and then go into a hotel lobby and kick it on the Internet. In Havana, the Parque Central Hotel has a really nice lobby and no one asks if you're a guest. Take refuge in the A/C, Internet and comforts of a beautiful hotel, without the high price tag.

Buying from the Wi-Fi Zone

If you can't be bothered lining up at the ETECSA to buy an Internet card for $2, you can head straight to the Wi-Fi zones to find people selling cards off the street. Fortunately for you, these lovely people have already gone to the trouble of lining up and purchasing the cards. All they ask in return is that you pay double the price...if not more! Hey, it's Cuba. Everyone has to earn a living.

You can try and haggle with them, but they're basically out to hustle unknowing tourists who don't know the real selling price. Out of haggling curiosity, the cheapest I got them down to was $3 for an hour card, but it takes a fair bit of Spanish and explaining to them that you know the original price. It's not worth the hassle unless the ETECSA store has closed or you really need to get online.

Connecting to an Internet Hot Spot in Cuba

The final way to find a connection in Cuba is to find someone hotspotting a connection in one of the public areas. Hotspotting from the locals is the most economical option and the one that a lot of Cubans use to cut back on the costs. It only costs $1 an hour, but it's not always the most reliable connection. In the few times we tried it, we kept having problems connecting, but it's worth a shot. Unfortunately, you're not able to hotspot from your own device (unless you're really tech-savvy). We tried to hotspot our phones to share a connection, but it kept bouncing us off the net.

To find someone hotspotting, you need to head to local plazas and keep an eye out for the masses of Cubans, generally in the evening, huddled around someone with a computer. Usually, they're running a program that allows them to share connections. Pay them $1 and they'll give you the password and access for an hour. The locals are really friendly about it and happy to help you get online. If you approach them and ask politely, they'll get you connected.

Pro Tip: It's reported that a free Internet connection is available at a location called the Paradero de Playa in Havana. The password is *abajoelbloqueo* (abolish the blockade). And although the connection isn't great, if you can find it, it can be a fun place to meet tech-savvy locals.

What Internet Means for Cuba

Although Cuba's recent embrace of the Internet might sound like a relief to Wi-Fi-addicted travelers, take a little time to appreciate just how much of a big deal this is to the locals, who for so many years have been restricted in their communication and accessibility to the outside world.

The Internet is opening up opportunities for them to reconnect with family who have been out of touch for years, if not decades. One of our favorite things to do was sit in the public parks and watch people get onto a video chat with family they rarely get to speak to, sometimes even for the first time. It was a truly incredible experience to witness. As the government slowly begins to loosen its control on communications, Cuba will continue to embrace the technological era with enthusiasm and readiness. But like all things in Cuba, it's difficult to predict how these changes will take form over the next few years.

Must-See Experiences

Visiting Cuba is all about having unique, authentic experiences that you can only find in this one-of-a-kind country. Here you'll find some absolute must-see or -do experiences on your next visit to Cuba. These experiences are the ones that will really stand out in your memory and enrich your understanding of Cuban life. And they aren't established tours that will cost you an arm and a leg. In fact, most of them are free. Some of them take just a little bit of confidence, maybe a bit of broken Spanish, and a desire of learn more about Cuba and its people. We have no doubt that you'll fall in love with the country just as we have.

Watch an Esquina Caliente

The literal Spanish translation is "hot corner" and it couldn't be more appropriately named. Things get hot on the *esquina calientes*, but not for the reasons you might be thinking of. This is strictly sport-related. At these spots, usually in public parks, you'll see groups of men huddled around a couple of people who are basically screaming at each other, debating everything from the latest sports results to the best player or team. Cubans love their sports, with baseball and football (soccer) being amongst the main discussion points.

The first time we came across an *esquina caliente* in Havana, we thought we'd stumbled across a massive argument. There was a group of at least twenty-five men circled around two guys who were yelling at each other. It looked more like a schoolyard fight than anything civilized. As we were preparing to witness a serious beat-down, one of the men threw his arms into the air in frustration, cursed at the other guy, and then left the circle. There was a wave of applause and the remaining man stood there with a smile on his face and a look of victory.

It's only then that we realized this mini-debate is more like the Cuban equivalent of a rap battle. Wit, charisma, and an ability to work the crowd into your favor are all skills needed if you're going to get your point across. It's not just what you're saying: It's how you're saying it. And if you've got the crowd on your side, the other guy doesn't stand a chance.

It might look intimidating, but don't let that put you off. Crowd around and watch, even if you don't have a clue what they're saying. This is a true example of Cuban passion and energy, especially when it comes to sports! For the location of one of our favorite *esquina calientes,* refer to the chapter: **The Authentic Havana Walking Guide**.

Smoking a Cigar and Drinking Rum

This shouldn't be a surprise to anyone planning a trip to Cuba, but the locals really enjoy their rum and cigars. Both rum and cigars are an iconic part of Cuban culture that must be experienced on your trip. Exactly how iconic is it? Okay, so you're not going to walk down every street and see ninety-year-old ladies puffing away on big old cigars, encased in a cloud of smoke, or men gathered around a table drinking straight rum from the bottle in the middle of the day. But Cubans sure do enjoy these things all the same. And truth be told, we've actually seen both of those things: They're just not as blatant as the postcards and Instagram shots might make them out to be.

Cuba is famous for its quality rum and cigars, and they don't disappoint. The rum is absolutely amazing and extremely well priced. For a 700 ml bottle of Havana Club you'll pay less than $4 USD, with the more premium aged bottles costing just a bit more. If you make it out to the Cuban countryside, you can see the miles upon miles of sugarcane growing along the highways. This is where it all starts…eventually ending over some ice, with a splash of cola and a pinch of lime, to make the perfect *Cuba Libre*. Whether you're enjoying a mojito at Hemingway's old hangout, El Floridita, or sharing a bottle down the Malecon with friends, it's always rum o'clock in Cuba.

Cigars, on the other hand, are a little pricier, with demand for Cuba's third biggest export raising the prices for everyone across the globe. Prices start at $2-3 for smaller cigars and go up to $20 and beyond for the bigger cigars. Cuba may be famous for their rum, but it's the cigars that really put them on the map. But don't fall for the oldest scam in Cuba by getting suckered into buying fake ones (see **Avoiding Scams**). Even though getting scammed at least once would be a pretty authentic Cuban experience, stick to the government stores to ensure quality.

Even if you're not a smoker (believe us, we're not at all), smoking a real Cuban cigar in Cuba over a glass of rum is an experience that will make you feel more Cuban than Fidel Castro himself. Just don't make the mistake that Jules did by getting carried away and smoking the whole thing. He ended up feeling sick all night and couldn't sleep from all the dizzy spells. Note to non-smokers: Go easy!

Go Salsa Dancing

Salsa music is an integral part of Cuban culture, just as much as the classic cars and Havana Club rum. You'll hear it pumping from crowded bars, blaring out of car speakers, and drifting from some unknown source down the cobblestone streets of Havana. You'll be walking down the street and suddenly you'll feel your shoulders start to roll a little, your fingers click, and your hips softly sway from side to side. You can't help it: It's infectious.

Salsa music drives Cuban culture. It's passionate, it's sexy, and Cubans are damn good at dancing it: from young kids in the street to oldies spinning and twirling around in the plazas. If you really want to amp it up, head to one of the pumping salsa clubs to see where the real magic happens. You'll find the Casa de Musica (House of Music) clubs in most big cities and they're full of tourists and locals alike.

Cuban-style salsa is unique because of the Afro-Caribbean influence it brings to the dance moves. There are fewer spins, with touches of rumba and lots of hip movements. Get ready to pop those hips and shake that booty! If you're not feeling confident enough to set the floor on fire, consider taking a few dance lessons to prep you up. You'll find salsa schools offering classes all over the country, helping stiff foreigners like ourselves loosen up those hips and sharpen up those foot skills. After taking only a few hours of classes, you'd be surprised how many steps you can pick up. Salsa really is about rhythm and repetition at the beginner level, so with a few steps under your belt, you can easily get away with a night of dancing. If all else fails, grab a local partner. They'll be able to guide you around the dance floor.

Here are some recommended dancing schools in Havana:

La Casa del Son

Salsabor A Cuba

Mi Salsa Cubana

Visit a Cigar Factory

Speaking of cigars, you really need to visit a local cigar-making factory. In some shops, you may see a local Cuban hand-rolling cigars on a little desk, but visiting a cigar factory is on another level. Slightly resembling something like a Communist labor camp, cigar factories in Cuba are a well-oiled machine, pumping out world class cigars by the thousands every single day.

One cigar factory we recommend is in the city of Santa Clara, about four hours east of Havana. It was an eye-opening experience to watch the Cuban workforce in its most authentic manner. Rows upon rows of desks lined up in unison, with all types of Cubans (young, old, male, and female) busily working away to what sounded like "inspirational" propaganda playing over the radio. There were posters on the wall displaying quotes from the revolution, as well as our favorite slogan from a big Fidel poster saying, "Those without jobs are the lazy people letting the country down." It's a simple reminder to the workers that being unemployed is not an option.

It's hard not to feel sorry for the workers as they work away at the desks all day rolling cigars, but they actually have a great job. They're among some of the best government-paid workers, with decent incentives for those who are good at what they do. Each cigar factory worker has their own unique identification number (labor camp much?) so the quality, or lack thereof, can be traced back to them.

List of Cigar Factories Available to Visit

Fabrica de Tabaco Partagas (Calle San Carlos, Havana): Originally situated across the street from the Capitol building, this cigar factory has now moved to corner of San Carlos and Penalver. It's the oldest cigar factory in Cuba. Established in 1845, it offers a brilliant insight into the industry. They don't sell tickets at the factory, so be sure to buy them before showing up. Tickets can be organized with a tour agency or at hotels. Before heading there, check to see if the factory has moved back to its original location after the renovations finish.

Romeo y Julieta Cigar Factory (Calle Padre Varela, Havana): You'll need a ticket to enter, either organized through a hotel or tour agency.

Santa Clara Cigar Factory: It's more low-key than the factories in Havana and a lot less touristy.

Watch a Dominoes Game

You can't experience real Cuba without watching, or getting involved with, a local game of dominoes. Cuba's favorite pastime is an experience that will definitely leave you with a new appreciation for what we assumed to be a pretty low-key, peaceful game. Like all things Cuba, a simple game of dominoes is played with passion and gusto that give the *esquina calientes* a run for their money. And speaking of money, if you stumble across a game with a few sneaky side wagers, expect to see the stakes (and emotions) raised even higher. At times, it's difficult to follow exactly what's going on because the players will be shouting at each other, slamming dominoes down on the table, and joking all at the same time. Whether it looks like they're friends or not, there is a definite sense of community among all players, which adds to the charm of Cuban culture.

Walking down the backstreets of Havana at dusk, after everyone has finished work, watching tables of people gathered around playing dominoes is a real insight into the authentic Cuban lifestyle. Without easy and affordable access to the Internet, computers, and TVs, Cubans have learned to preserve the ancient art of actually talking to each other…in person. For the location of one of the best street corners to catch a dominoes game, check **The Authentic Havana Walking Guide** chapter

Visit a Cuban Barbershop

Visiting a local barber in Cuba is a really unique way to see the normal, day-to-day Cuban life that happens outside of the tourist areas. In Cuba, a barbershop isn't just a place to get a shave and a cut, it's a place to hang out with your buddies and chat about anything from cars and sports, to women and politics. Cutthroat razor shaves, pictures of girls hanging from the wall, and the strong scent of cologne make up the basic fundamentals of a Cuban barbershop. Generally only frequented by men, local barbershops give you the full Cuba experience. You're in for a real treat with this experience, fellas.

Not only is the experience super-authentic, but cuts are ridiculously cheap! Like all things in Cuba, the price depends on your Spanish and negotiating skills, but you can expect to pay between $1.5-$3 to get a full razor shave and haircut. They'll give you the latest Latin look (which is pretty much your only option) and sharpen up those sideburns. If you're feeling particularly Cuban, ask the barber to shave a couple of horizontal lines into your hair like the locals.

Now ladies, unless you're sporting a bit of facial hair, you might be limited in your options at the barbershop. You could always get your hair cut, but they're pretty rough around the edges, so most ladies stick to the beauty salons that offer a little more care and finesse. By all means, pop your head in to grab a peek, though. Like all Cubans, the beauty shop ladies are super-friendly. One alternative option for the ladies is getting a manicure from a little pop-up nail salon inside someone's house.

Visit the Malecon at Night

No trip to Havana is complete without going down to the Malecon (esplanade waterfront) on a Friday or Saturday night to have a drink with the locals and to listen to local musicians strumming away on a guitar. Formally known as Avenida de Maceo (named after the famous war hero Antonio Maceo), this esplanade stretches for miles along the Havana coast, but is best visited between the streets of Padre Varela and Galiano.

The action usually doesn't kick off until at least 8-9 p.m., but slowly, as the night goes on, the party starts to pick up. As you walk the Malecon, you'll find all sorts of different people enjoying the festivities: some singing and strumming away on guitars to Cuban classics and new pop songs alike, some groups with speakers busting out reggaeton or salsa hits, or just people sitting around and talking over a bottle of rum. The best part about the Malecon is that is doesn't discriminate in its crowd. Anyone and everyone is welcome to join in the fun.

Cubans love the opportunity to mingle with foreigners outside the usual tourist routes, so heading down the Malecon at night gives you the chance to make some local friends. Meeting some of the university students, who often speak good English, is a great way to get a youth's perspective on what's going on in Cuba at the moment. They'll have the old historical facts that have been drummed into them since a very young age, as well as the contemporary thoughts that are circulating among young academics concerning Cuba's future. And there's no need to be worried about your safety, even at two or three in the morning, you can feel confident cruising down the Malecon. Check out **Safety in Cuba** to see a full explanation.

Finding Bootleg Beer

The beer is Cuba is already pretty cheap. For a dollar, you can buy a can of the local drop in the street. In restaurants and bars, they'll up the price a bit, but it's pretty manageable. Kicking back with a beer in the park or plaza is a great way to watch Cuban life go by, but if you want to really mix it up with the locals and experience Cuban homebrew, you've got to track down one of the *camionetas de cerveza* (beer trucks).

You can't find them everywhere (we only came across them in Trinidad and Matanzas), but if you do, put aside an hour to drink some of the cheapest beer you'll ever find with a host of interesting characters. It's BYO-container, no matter what shape or size it comes in, and you'll see people drinking out of mugs, old soda bottles, or even REI water bottles. It's no fancy craft beer, but honestly, it hits the spot. It's the stock standard international beer recipe that every country seems to brew, and at less than 10 cents for half a liter, you really can't complain too much. Outside these beer trucks, they tend to set up tables and chairs, so you can pull up a seat and hang with the locals.

Get Invited into a Local's House

By far, the best way to see authentic Cuba is to be invited into the house of a local. It might sound like a pretty difficult thing to do, especially if you don't speak a lot of Spanish, but Cubans are incredibly hospitable and always opening the door to family and strangers alike. Sure, if you stay at *casa particulares*, you'll get the opportunity to see inside a Cuban family's house, but getting invited in by a stranger off the street is a super-unique way to see authentic Cuba. The casas, as great as they are, have had hundreds of guests before you, so some of the families are a little worn out from tourists. On our 2016 trip, we felt that there was less excitement from some of the hosts. It's inevitable that this will happen, though, as the *casa particulares* continue to get busier.

During our travels in Cuba, we had several opportunities to hang out with locals, and each one presented such a unique and interesting story. There was the time we were invited in for coffee and sweets by an older woman in Trinidad after admiring her painting from the window. We had a fascinating conversation with her husband about his time working in the Ministry of Economics, where he was one of the first people in all of Cuba to use a computer back in the 1970s. Or there was the time Jules was invited into the house of a lady in Havana to have an hour-long lesson about Cuba's Santeria culture, sacrificing pigeons and goats, and the crossover of Catholicism and traditional Afro-Caribbean beliefs. Where else in the world could you find something like this?

Cuba Travel Hacks

The following ten Cuba travel hacks, along with the tips and tricks from *The Authentic Cuba Travel Guide,* will continue to help you travel deeper, cheaper, and more authentically in Cuba. We include our best packing, budgeting, and cultural hacks, so you can have a truly memorable experience traveling through Cuba.

Packing Hacks

Although Cuba is generally a pretty budget-friendly destination, the trade embargo with the US means that items not made in Cuba are imported from far off countries. This means that shopping is limited, so you need to ensure you pack all your essentials before taking off. It's not that you won't find them (although in some cases, you won't), but if you do, they'll be five or six times the normal price, or possibly even more, depending on the scarcity of the item.

Toiletries

Although it's not like the old days where you have to bring your own toilet paper, you should stock up on certain items before arriving. Decent toiletries like shampoo, conditioner, deodorant, and sunscreen are difficult to find and expensive if you do. We highly recommend bringing razors, as they can be ridiculously pricey in Cuba. We saw Gillette razors for 25 CUC (yep, that's $25 USD!). On the flip side, we saw disposable razors sold on the street for 25 cents, but that was just by chance after going razor-less for two weeks when we couldn't find a cheap one in the store. It's definitely worth your time to investigate where you can find the cheapest prices before overpaying for items. Otherwise, prepare to go hairy!

Dietary Requirements

Vegetarians and vegans may want to consider packing snacks to have for emergency tummy rumbles. Vitamins or supplements might also be a good idea if you plan on eating on a budget. While the street pizzas may fill your stomach, they have low to no nutritional value. Is cheese a vitamin? Packing daily vitamins can help keep your energy up and your body happy. The same goes for travelers with specific dietary requirements or allergies. I don't think "dairy-free" has made it into the Cuban vocabulary yet.

Bottled Water

We don't recommend drinking the tap water in Cuba. Although bottled water is pretty easy to find, it can be a bit expensive and the plastic is terrible for the environment. In tourist areas, bottled water will be marked up, sometimes costing $1-$2 per bottle. We recommend bringing some sort of water filter, so you can drink directly from the tap. We love our LifeStraw Go bottles that have a filter directly in the water bottle, making it incredibly easy to fill up wherever we are. This can also be a great conversation starter if you ask locals to fill up your bottle. Chances are, they'll be more than happy to oblige and even ask you to stick around for a chat. We've also used the SteriPEN UV filter on previous trips and it has worked well. The security at the *Museo de la Revolución* freaked out big time when they saw us swirling around a fluorescent light in front of their treasured museum, however, so be discreet.

Clothing

Cuba can get extremely hot, so check the climate during the time of year that you're traveling. Thin, cotton clothing is usually the best for hot, humid weather. Sporadic rain can happen all year round, so a light rain jacket may be useful, or you may be able to borrow or buy an umbrella. As mentioned in **Traveling as a Solo Female**, Cubans, especially the youth, do not dress very conservatively. Tight, short dresses and tank tops are common for women, and men sometimes walk around without shirts. In most countries, we advise travelers to dress a bit on the modest side, but in Cuba, feel free to strut your stuff! Chances are, there will always be locals wearing less than you are, unless you walk around naked!

Adapters and Power

In Cuba, you'll find Type A and Type B power plugs used throughout the country. It is quite common to find Type A plugs in older casas, so you'll need a power adapter for most foreign cords. Most of the power supply in Cuba is at 110 volts, although some modern hotels and casas have dual voltage and provide 220 volts.

Budget Hacks

As we've mentioned in detail in **Budgeting for Cuba: From Low to High,** Cuba travel can be as cheap or as expensive as you want. But if you are looking to save some pennies, here are a few foolproof tips for keeping your costs down.

The Carta Baja

The biggest tip for staying on a budget in Cuba is to try and do as the locals do. If you eat and drink at local spots, you'll be eating for a fraction of the cost compared to the tourist places. But what happens if the local and the tourist spots are actually the same place? You might be wondering, how do the locals afford to eat here, or how do they charge different people different prices? Easily: with two different menus. That's right: Some restaurants will actually have two different printed menus depending on if you're a foreigner or a local. This may seem completely unfair, but the truth is, even budget backpackers have more money to spend than locals. The only way to get around the system is to be upfront with the restaurateurs. If you see a mix of locals and tourists at the restaurant, ask for the *carta baja* (low menu). You can explain to them that the prices are too high for you, or that you usually pay for things in the local currency. You can also tell them that you're a student. Any of these statements will get the point across that you're on a budget. If they do have a *carta baja*, they may choose to give it to you or they may not. There's also a chance they have one menu for everyone, so don't press too hard. If they do give you the local's menu, be gracious and don't flash it around to the other tourists. You've got the golden ticket and you don't want it taken away.

Moneda Nacional

You'll get the best deals in Cuba if you use the local currency wherever you can. That doesn't mean you can pay for your 25 CUC car ride around Havana with 25 CUP of local currency...that's not gonna fly. However, the places that do accept the CUP are the cheapest. Many places will accept both CUP and CUC, but chances are they won't give you the best exchange rate if you're paying CUC for a CUP purchase.

Haggling

At first, you may feel uncomfortable haggling in a country with such low wages because you certainly don't want to cheat anyone out of a fair wage. But rest assured, that this is a part of the tourist/Cuban culture and locals will only ever accept a price that makes sense for them. They're not going to undercut themselves by accepting prices that are too low. Plus, Cuba receives enough tourism every day that they can just hawk their wares to the next tourist if you're being too much of a scrooge. Haggling in Cuba is definitely expected and accepted, especially for street crafts, tourist services, and at the market. Remember, though, that 99 percent of the handicrafts and clothing that you see will be made in the country, much of it handmade. These aren't factory-made knock-offs from China. So don't be offended if a shopkeeper isn't willing to budge on the price; it's possible they've made their items personally by hand.

Culture Hacks

The Cuban lifestyle is in many ways similar to other Latin American countries, however, there are certain cultural customs that may be a bit confusing to Cuba newbies. Here are a couple you should be aware of.

To Kiss or Not to Kiss?

It's customary to give a light kiss on the left cheek when meeting new people or greeting acquaintances. This isn't just between female-female or male-male; even some men will kiss each other on the cheek. I wouldn't rush in to give your taxi driver a big smooch—it's usually reserved for good friends only. Some people may shake your hand, so just go with their lead.

Ultimo

Inevitably, you'll find yourself standing in line somewhere in Cuba. Government-run institutions often mean slow service and lots of waiting. Upon first glance, it may appear that there's no order to a group standing around a counter. If you join the mess without knowing your place in line, you can expect to be waiting for a long time, but the locals will always know exactly who's next in line. To secure your spot, simply walk up and ask *"ultimo?"* This directly translates to "last" and basically means, "Who's last in line?" Someone will put his or her hand up and you'll go after that person. Don't worry about who is ahead of who, just remember that when that person goes, you're after them. Remember to be assertive because some cheeky locals will have no problem cutting you in the line.

Commissions

As mentioned previously, Cubans don't earn much from their jobs. That's why they look for little ways to supplement their income wherever they can. One way is to take a commission for bringing in clients to other businesses. A common one comes from locals who will spot you on the street and ask if you have a hotel room or *casa particular*. If you say no, they'll take you to the house of a friend and often get a small commission for bringing you in. Sometimes their commission will be extra on top of the price, so you need to factor that in. This is common for accommodation, restaurants, and tours all throughout Cuba. Although it seems a bit sneaky, this is a normal way for locals to earn some extra money. As long as they're not taking you for a ride, this can be a pretty handy way to organize things because the locals know best. If you're not comfortable with this, simply say "no thanks" to anyone approaching you in the street with offers.

The Authentic Havana Walking Guide

Ask anyone who has traveled to Cuba and they're likely to tell you Havana was their favorite part. It's one of the most unique places in the entire world, and everything about this capital city just screams "authentic Cuba," from the charming rustic architecture and cobblestoned streets, to the old classic cars, vibrant nightlife, and diversity of people. It's an absolute must-see city while visiting Cuba.

For travelers flying in and out of Havana airport, it's easy to stay a couple of days at the start or end of your trip to explore the city. If you're flying into Cuba through another airport, we really recommend taking the time to spend at least a few days in Havana. Personally, we'd suggest three to four days minimum to really get a feel for it, but as always, the longer you stay, the more you'll get out of it.

Here are our top twenty locations to experience the real Cuba. In *The Authentic Havana Walking Guide,* you'll find everything from hole-in-the-wall restaurants to unique activities, interesting places, and everything else original Cuba. You can match the number of the location to the map provided in this chapter.

Most of the tourist activity happens in Habana Vieja (Old Havana), but all you need to do is wander away from of the main tourist zone to avoid expensive restaurants, fake-cigar hawkers, and overpriced car rides. Use this map to see the *authentic* Cuban lifestyle:

1. El Coubre train station. If you're looking for a long-distance trip through Cuba, this is the station currently in operation in 2016 (the main central station is under renovation and set to open in early 2017). It's an experience and a half (albeit a little difficult and uncomfortable), but one that is authentic Cuba through and through!

2. Vibrant Cuban culture comes to life in the afternoons around Picota and Leonor Pérez. Here you'll find everything from kids playing baseball on the street and kicking around the football to women braiding hair and men sipping from bootleg bottles of rum.

If you've purchased a paperback copy of this book and would like an electronic version of the map please visit: http://bit.ly/authentic-havana

3. La Feria is an artesian market that sells every type of Cuban souvenir you could think of. If you're looking to purchase a few Cuban keepsakes, this is the place

to go, but bear in mind that it's populated by tourists and the prices reflect that. Be prepared to haggle and don't worry about offending the vendors: It's all part of the game. One great feature of this market is the selection of artwork if you're looking to pick up a few pieces. Plus, they can pack and wrap everything for you on the spot. You can even have it sent home, if you trust the Cuban postal system. There's also a money exchange spot if you're in the area and have your cash and passport. The line is a lot shorter than those in the center of Old Havana on Calle Obispo.

4. A new craft beer brewery, called Cerveceria Antiguo Almancen del la Madera y El Tobaco, has recently opened next to La Feria. It's the same company (run by the government) as Factoria Plaza Vieja that can be found in Plaza Vieja. You'll find a little bit of a better selection than the beers on the street and can choose from light, cloudy, or dark beers. They also have a bar that can mix up your favorite cocktails. Mugs of beer cost 2 CUC, and there is a small selection of food available if you get hungry. There are tables inside facing a stage, as well as outside facing towards the harbor. It's not a sensational view, but it's nice to get the breeze on a particularly hot day.

Music groups play your favorite Cuban salsa hits sporadically throughout the day, so bring some small change to offer a tip.

5. Where to find a mean game of street dominoes! Every night, just outside the little park on the corner of Merced and Picota, you can find a table of rowdy men and many more onlookers. Dominoes slam down on the table and men cheer like it's a big football match. Games take on even more enthusiasm, shouting, and hollering after a few pesos go down on the table.

6. **Ilé Aché Hostel** (Calle Damas n° 858, entre Merced y Paula | +53 5 8183989. Dorm beds for 10 CUC a night. Offers a nice friendly vibe, a kitchen to cook in, and includes a DIY breakfast of eggs, bread, and fruit. A great option if you're traveling solo in Cuba and don't want to pay for a casa by yourself. They offer discounts for longer stays and only have a dozen beds at the moment, so it's always best to check ahead of time.

7. On the corner of Merced and Cuba, outside the front of Iglesia Merced (Merced Church), you can find evening games of baseball with the local children of

the neighborhood. Occasionally they'll be playing with sticks and whatever makeshift ball they've been able to create, and it's awesome to see their creativity and passion for the sport.

8. Along Jesús María, you can find local barbers that will give you the full treatment for a couple of CUC. You'll get a traditional Latino cut, a fresh shave, and some entertaining conversation. Go more for the experience than the final product.

9. The best guava pastries we found all over Havana came from a small shop near the corner of Picota and Luz, across from the Igelsia y Convento de Belen. On the street, look for a yellow house that also operates as a little *tienda* (shop). The older lady speaks a little English and is happy to have chat if you stick around.

10. In the afternoons and evenings, you can find street games of football (soccer) between the neighborhood boys (aged fifteen to twenty-five-ish). They play in an open area near the corner of Cuba and Sol, adjacent to the Convento de Santa Clara (Santa Clara Convent). The games are lighthearted and fun, but

they still take it seriously. You'll be surprised how good some of these guys are!

11. This place was one of our favorite street food restaurants in Habana Vieja (Old Havana). It's one house up from the corner of Mercedes and Sol. If you're walking up Mercedes towards Plaza Vieja, it'll be on the left side. There's a small doorway going into a courtyard-type arrangement of tables, or you can order from the window to the left. If you're looking for a complete meal, you'll find whole plates of food for only 25 CUP (1 CUC) that include meat or fish with rice and vegetables. If you're just looking for something on the go, then grab a *batido* (fruit milkshake) and egg sandwich—the best in town!

12. Yes, they're in the middle of the main tourist area, but the secondhand stalls that surround Plaza de Armas on Calle Obispo are something else. Visiting this place is like taking a trip back in time to a 1960s yard sale. These vendors sell everything from old books and posters to original watches from in the USSR and revolutionary memorabilia. But just because Cuba is cheap, don't expect any massive discounts on the highly prized items. Some of the watches being sold

are priced in the hundreds of dollars! Either way, it's definitely worth taking a wander around the stalls and imagining Cuba many decades ago.

Tourist Zone

In this section, you'll find all the usual touristy things that you see in the guidebooks, TripAdvisor, and so on. The main walking street of Calle Obispo is where all the action takes place. Other popular streets include Mercedes and San Ignacio as they lead down into Plaza Vieja, as well Oficinos as it goes down to Plaza de San Francisco. It's worth spending some time exploring, but try to limit the time spent on these streets because they don't represent real Cuban lifestyle and culture. If you want to change money, buy Internet cards (see **How to Find Internet in Cuba**), and check out a tourist bar, you can pop past, but otherwise, the main Cuba action happens outside of this grid.

13. A classic Cuban dive bar, called Bar 66 or something similar. Located on Calle Refugio, in between Paseo de Marti and Morro. If you're turning the corner from Paseo de Marti, walking towards the Malecon. It'll be on the right side about three-quarters of the way up. In this bar, you can expect to find a couple of drunk men passed out over a table and a bottle of rum, old salsa tunes blaring from a static TV, and lots of

friendly service and conversation...and that's just at 1 p.m. Stick around for the evening crowd if you want some real liveliness.

14. The Havana Malecon! You'll find lots of action most nights, but especially on the weekends. At any time between 5 p.m. to late, you will meet people all along the Malecon, but this particular section (between Padre Varela and Galiano) gets the most activity. More on the Malecon in **Must-See Experiences**.

15. The Parque Central Hotel is best place to use Internet in all of Havana. Why bother sitting on the hot street in the gutter, when you can sit on a couch in nice air conditioning for free? You don't even need to be a guest there. More info about Internet and locations under **How to Find Internet in Cuba**.

16. The best place in Havana to find an *esquina caliente* (hot corner) is in Parque Central. In the middle of the park, in the evenings, you'll find a load of men going crazy at each other. Don't know what an *esquina calienta* is? Check under **Must-See Experiences**.

17. An awesome little unnamed spot to eat that does a cheap (25 CUP – 1 CUC) plate of rice, beans, and salad for the more vegetarian inclined. It's on a nice quiet pedestrian street that gets some foot traffic, but nothing like the hordes of tourists on the walking street Calle Obispo. This street is like the local equivalent to Calle Obispo. It has shops, restaurants, and bars, but very few foreigners frequent them, so it's a nice spot to explore.

18. This park area, Parque de la Fraternidad, is smack-bang in the middle of the local transport network, is surprisingly chill throughout the day. There are benches and shade, perfect for escaping the midday heat, and it's a nice spot to kick back and watch Cuba go about its daily business.

19. At this spot on Amistad, a lot of local *gua-guas* (public buses) pass through. You can get a bus that goes close to the airport (within a few kilometers) for only 0.4 CUP (1 cent USD). You can also get buses to other parts of town and to other transport stops that will take you to cities in other provinces for a fair price. The schedules and routes are confusing, so it's best to check and double-check which bus you need to get.

Cubans are super-friendly and will help you find where you need to go if you're polite and can speak a little Spanish.

20. Another local tourist hub for picking up a share ride, true Cuban style. The exact location is a few streets back from where the local *gua-guas* depart on Amistad (see 19), but all around the area, you'll find cars and trucks filling up and heading out to spots all over Cuba. You'll have to negotiate prices, but it shouldn't be too difficult if other locals are around. They'll help you find the right car and price. The ride will take longer than anticipated, and you'll be squished in, but it'll be a real experience traveling like the locals. Plus, it's cheap! Expect to pay about 1 CUC per hour, as a rough price, but it can be even lower than that depending on how many people the driver can take.

For a few days in Havana, these spots will really help enrich your experience of authentic Cuba, as well save you a lot of money! If you check out the local restaurants, accommodation, and transport, you're bound to save hundreds in costs, as well as get a much better insight into authentic Cuba than the average tourist.

Christine Williams & Julian Hatfield

Thank You!

You've now reached the end of **The Authentic Cuba Travel Guide**. We truly hope you have an enriched sense of excitement and enthusiasm for what lies ahead! Everything in this book is tried, tested and authentically Cuba, so if you follow our advice you're about to have one amazing trip! Before you run off and book your trip to Cuba we do ask you to read ahead for another 2 minutes.

What next? Well, we hope you've enjoyed The Authentic Cuba Travel Guide so much that you want to go and share it with all your friends. Here's an easy link that you can share on your Facebook, Twitter, Instagram, in an email and any other social media platform you use: **http://bit.ly/CubaBook**

Leave Us a Review

If you loved our book and found it helpful we'd be forever thankful if you were able to leave us a review on Amazon. Simply go to the link of the Amazon store closest to your country and leave us a review.

US Amazon - http://amzn.to/29bZo6x

Canada Amazon - http://amzn.to/295XG44

UK Amazon - http://amzn.to/29dP2F9

If you do have any feedback regarding the book, mistakes, outdated information, or anything else, please don't hesitate to get in contact with us. We're always open to feedback, both positive and negative, and look to continue improving this book for the months to come.

Make a Donation

If you thought the book was so good that it should have been valued higher, or if you went to Cuba and literally saved hundreds, why not drop a few CUC back into our travel fund? It helps keep us on the road, providing great content for other future travelers. All donations can be made through PayPal to the following email address: christinewilliams87@gmail.com

Keep It Real

Lastly we want to ask you to respect the effort that has gone into researching, writing, editing and producing this guide for you. Please do not share it with anyone who has not purchased a copy. As travel bloggers we already give away 99% of our content for free and do not ask for contributions from our readers. We also don't junk up your viewing experience with messy advertisements, so this guide is one of the few ways that we can make money and continue providing useful information to travelers all over the world.

Christine Williams & Julian Hatfield

About the Authors

Christine Williams and Julian Hatfield are the authors of *The Authentic Cuba Travel Guide* and professional travel bloggers at **Don't Forget To Move** (http://dontforgettomove.com). For the last six years, they've been traveling the world, becoming established experts on everything travel. Their biggest goal is to inspire people to see the world and to help them get the most out of their travels, regardless of budget, time, or previous travel experience.

In 2013, they traveled to Cuba for the first time and completely fell in love with the country's charm and vibrancy. Upon returning from their trip, they noticed a lack of relevant and accurate information on traveling to Cuba. After collating all of their experiences on Don't Forget To Move, they quickly became a trusted resource on Cuban travel, with their content receiving hundreds of thousands of page views.

After countless reader emails, questions, and inquiries, they decided to go back to Cuba in 2016 to continue their research and provide more up-to-date information. On their most recent trip to Cuba, in April 2016, Christine and Julian were able to experience a different version of Cuba, one more technologically advanced and open to more travelers, namely Americans. After this trip, Christine and Julian noticed an even greater need for accurate information online, as well as a guide for travelers who want to experience the *real* Cuba. So they created this book!

Printed in Great Britain
by Amazon